JEFF HARLOW

ACT3
Facilitator Guide

Discover God's Calling for the
Third Stage of Life

JEFF HARLOW

ACT3
Facilitator Guide

Discover God's Calling for the
Third Stage of Life

ACT3MINISTRY.COM

EPIPHANY
PUBLISHING

Published in Indianapolis, Indiana by Epiphany Publishing, LLC.

Unless otherwise indicated, all Scripture quotations are taken from the Holy Bible, New International Version (NIV). © 1973, 1978, 1984 by International Bible Society. Used by permission. All rights reserved worldwide.

Scripture quotations marked NKJV are taken from the New King James Version®. Copyright © 1982 by Thomas Nelson. Used by permission. All rights reserved.

Scriptures marked NASU are taken from the NEW AMERICAN STANDARD UPDATED (NASU): Scripture taken from the NEW AMERICAN STANDARD UPDATED BIBLE®, copyright©, 1995 by The Lockman Foundation. Used by permission.

Excerpt from *The Velveteen Rabbit: Or How Toys Become Real* by Williams, Margery. London, George H. Doran Company, 1922, is in the public domain.

The *Calling Star*™ symbol is a registered trademark of ACT3. All rights reserved.

For information about special discounts available for bulk purchases, sales promotions, fund-raising, and educational needs, contact Epiphany Publishing Sales at sales@epiphanypublishing.us.

ISBN 978-1946093103 (Facilitator Guide paperback)
ISBN 978-1946093127 (Facilitator Guide hardback)
ISBN 978-1946093110 (Participant Guide paperback)

First printing in 2019. 08/01/2021 version.
This book was printed in the United States of America.

Epiphany Publishing
P.O. Box 36814
Indianapolis, IN 46236
www.epiphanypublishing.us
info@epiphanypublishing.us

How to Use this Facilitator Guide

Thank you for fulfilling the critical role of Discovery Team Facilitator for your local ACT3 initiative. You are foundational to the first step of the Discovery journey designed to guide people who are searching for what is next in their life.

This facilitator guide is a companion handbook to the ACT3 Participant Guide. It is intended to guide facilitators in helping others discover the masterpiece that God has created them to be, and to provide a pathway forward to connect them to the works that God prepared in advance for them to do.

This guide contains the full text of the Participant Guide as well as supplemental materials needed to successfully facilitate a Discovery Growth Group. This includes summaries, facilitation tips, commentary to augment the original material, and ample space for your personal notes. An exact copy of each page of the Participant Guide is included at the top left of the page. This lets you as the facilitator see exactly what the participants are seeing, complete with their original page numbers.

To help keep the two guides separate, the content of the Participant Guide is depicted in a serif font (which looks like this), while the content of the Facilitator Guide is depicted in a sans serif font like you see here.

Facilitators should make a point to always spend thoughtful personal preparation time with this guide prior to the sessions. This is the key to building confidence with the material and credibility as a facilitator. Should this material be team-facilitated, there should be a senior facilitator, and the assignments of who's-covering-what should be made well in advance of the session.

This content was designed for a 2:15 session. It can readily be reduced to 2 hours and start at any time of the day.

While facilitators can certainly substitute personal illustrations for the metaphors or stories contained in this material, every effort should be made to maintain alignment with the intent of the segment.

In addition to the original content of the Participant Guide, the following elements are also included in this guide:

WEEK AT A GLANCE – Each section opens with a short overview of the week's outcomes and agenda. This includes a summary of the activities as well as a suggested timeframe. Use this to quickly orient yourself to the structure of the material.

TEACHING POINTS – These sections include answers to the fill-in-the-blank portions of the Participant Guide, instructions for the group, and commentary to enhance your understanding of the material.

MY STORY – This is a space provided for you to outline your own personal examples that are relevant to the section. Stories are powerful and affecting, and they will often capture the attention of everyone in the room. By sharing open, thoughtful insights about your own journey, you encourage the group to do the same. Follow the prompts in the My Story sections to draft out your own illustrations.

My Story:
Space for you to write out your story

TIMEFRAME – This icon identifies how long the group should spend on a given section. Deviating from these timeframes means the group will likely go over (or under) the recommended amount of time. Write in the start and end time to help you keep an eye on the clock.

⧗	**10 Min**	Start Time: End Time:

BIG IDEA – This box contains a concise summary of the main concept of the section. The Big Idea is there to help anchor the stories, questions, and discussions you facilitate as you lead the group through the material. If time starts running short or the discussions begin to go off track, lead the group back to the Big Idea and drive that point home.

BIG IDEA

The section's big idea will go here

DESIRED OUTCOME – Each facilitator has his or her own style, and each Discovery Growth Group has its own needs and group dynamics. The Desired Outcome summarizes where the facilitators should lead the group, regardless of the path they take to get there. Reference the Desired Outcome to get a sense of what you should seek to accomplish in each section.

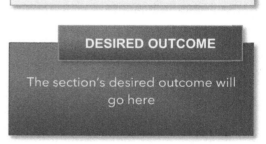

DESIRED OUTCOME

The section's desired outcome will go here

Thank you again for helping the participants of your Discovery Growth Groups rediscover who they are and how their calling takes shape in the 3rd stage of life. May God bless you for the support and guidance you offer to them.

Blessings,
Jeff Harlow

Contents

Introduction

If an eagle that had just caught an updraft for a soar could talk, don't you know it would scream, "*I was made for this!*" If an apple tree loaded with flawless fruit could talk, don't you know it would whisper, "*I was made for this!*" If a child's mind could be read while playing a favorite game with his or her best friends, don't you know the words would shout, "*I was made for this!*"

It was with you in mind that this guide was produced. It was for one purpose that this process was developed. At the heart of this study is the hope that you will confirm what makes you the Master's masterpiece and discover opportunities to engage at your fullest potential. Every effort was driven by the urge for you to experience the profound joy of partnering with the King to impact an outcome your world desperately needs. We want your breath to be taken by reflexively thinking, "*I was made for this!*" You can't allow yourself to exhale your last breath bereft of that mountaintop experience.

The bar has been set too low for 3rd Stagers. The opportunities to engage have tended towards the menial for those possessing the most experience. The world needs you more than you know. God has made you for a time such as this. Life was designed to be a crescendo, but you have to decide to hit the high note.

Our highest hope is that with each lesson and every assessment, the foggy mirror will clear and reflect the beautiful you, the only you God has ever made. It is our deepest desire that with every conversation the lights will brighten the pathway that leads you to your calling. We want to be in the crowd cheering when Jesus embraces you in heaven and says loudly enough for everyone to hear: *Well done!*

Enjoy rediscovering your calling,
Jeff, Becky, and Courtney

ACT3 Participant Guide

How to Use This Guide

Icons—Explanations of the icons used in this content are listed at the end of this segment.

Participant Information—Contact information for each participant of our group has been included as available. You are also given ample space to jot personal facts that participants share. Getting to know and becoming known is a huge advantage in this Discovery process. You may have a new close friend that you will meet for the first time in this Discovery Group.

Group Dialogue—Your experience will be enriched by the conversations that are directed within the times of sharing. Those conversations will take place in three different types of structured environments: At times, the conversations will include the entire group. Some of the discussions will take place in smaller clusters comprised of others at your table or those sitting closest to you. Finally, the deepest sharing will take place in the personal settings of 2-3 participants.

Scripture Study—Your Discovery process is undergirded with Scripture. The confidence you can have in the power of this process is that it is based solidly on scriptural principles and Biblical Truth.

Assessment Tools—A personal strengths assessment will be provided separately. The **Spiritual Gifts Assessment** (p. 47) is embedded within the content. If you have taken a spiritual gifts assessment in the past year, feel free to use those findings. If it has been longer than that, then your time would be well spent to take an assessment again. Your discovery guide will support you for your time study, whether you use the Excel tool supplied by your guide, or use the manual tool (p. 94).

Calling Star—Your *Calling Star* (p. xiii) is the composite picture of the masterpiece God has made you to be. Don't wait until the last minute to distill the information and input it into the appropriate points of the star. Keep it current. Enjoy the process of watching it come together.

ix

ACT3 Participant Guide

Going Deeper—Our meetings are fast-paced and flush with rich content. Time is a factor. Starting on time is imperative. Even then, powerful truths are left for you to personally pursue. When there is more content than time, we supply a section at the end of the chapter entitled Going Deeper. THIS IS NOT LIKE EXTRA CREDIT! It serves to enhance your experience and strengthen your grip on the Discovery process. Though the studies are optional, we believe you will find them invaluable.

Subject Experts—Sometimes you may be given the opportunity of a guest facilitator, particularly trained to facilitate the subject and discussion of the evening.

Serving Exploration Worksheet—Other than your *Calling Star* itself, no worksheet deserves more attention and necessitates more self-honesty. These two tools are the heart and soul of your coaching experience during Week 6. Make the **Serving Exploration Worksheet** (p. 99) your friend.

Serving Coach—You will be assigned a serving coach to help you assimilate and leverage the information, as well as make observations and add insights to your *Calling Star*.

Homework—Your ACT3 discovery experience is an investment in your future. God will honor your commitment to the pursuit of self-assessment and the opportunities to serve in alignment with your calling. Homework is no small part of this experience. When asked to pray for others, pray. Also, know they are praying for you. When asked to complete worksheets, give yourself fully to it. God will not miss the moment to speak to you through these tools and clarify who you are through these assessments.

MAXIMIZING YOUR ACT3 DISCOVERY EXPERIENCE

Prayer—There is no one like the Master to explain His masterpiece. Invite Him to talk. Commit to listening.

Preparation—All group members should commit to prepare in advance by working through the Homework assigned for each week. **You will not get where you want to go without completing the assessments and assigned worksheets**. There simply are no shortcuts to this experience. You should complete your assignments reflectively and prayerfully. Mastery of this material and a solid grasp of the aggregate picture that your *Calling Star* paints will yield massive rewards for the rest of your life. Don't cheat the process, yourself, or the people and plans you were designed to serve.

Scripture—Expect the Word to be relevant to you. Take the time to read the scriptures in each lesson, both before and after the lesson. Open your heart to the personal insights afforded by the texts of the lesson.

Questions—Submit to the power of a question. The questions of this study are designed to probe deeply and point boldly to issues you are wise to consider.

x

Authenticity is an absolute must. You must make this a genuine experience. Appropriate respect for the questions will take you where you might not otherwise go, but need to.

Discussion—When discussion within the group is open, overcome the temptation to be silent. Saying what you think out loud becomes a kind of declaration that leaves an impression on your soul. And someone else may need to hear what you think. Share your insights from the assessments without hesitation. You are surrounded by people who want you to succeed—people who are fascinated to hear your story. Share the meaningful insights that you discover. When it's time for one-on-one sharing, be prayerful about who that person will be. If you're married, talk through what you've learned at home. While you're in the group setting, give God a chance to expand your friend circles. Look for a same-gender person whose talk seems to resonate with you. Expect God to use your partner to confirm what you think and clarify those things about which you are uncertain.

Attendance—These lessons are designed to be a sequential experience. Make a personal commitment to attend every session with your peers. Because this is a shared experience, your friends are depending on your consistency to attend. Missing more than one will subvert the process. Of course, emergencies cannot be helped. If a 2nd lesson must be missed, please talk through the challenges with your facilitator. It is better to repeat the process than to shortchange it.

Arrival—We advise you to arrive 10 minutes before the scheduled start of a meeting. Feeling rushed will affect the experience. The informality of those few minutes before the meeting creates a rich environment in which to get comfortable with your peers and to develop new friendships. That extra 10 minutes will prove to be a cheap price for a valuable return.

DISCOVERY CONTENT ICONS

CALLING STAR highlights one of the primary personal traits that form the aggregate picture of the masterpiece God has designed you to be.

DISCUSSION highlights dialogue among the entire discovery group. It can be times of personal introduction or group interaction on designated issues. Except for introductions, personal sharing is encouraged, but not required.

TABLE TALK highlights dialogue among subsets of the Discovery Growth Group. Sharing is highly encouraged at a cursory level.

xi

ACT3 Participant Guide

 PERSONAL SHARING highlights dialogue between 2-3 participants at a deeper level. Same gender pairing is preferred to encourage potential accountability friendships.

 SCRIPTURE highlights Bible passages foundational to the teaching points and personal assessments.

 CONCEPT IMAGERY highlights object lessons used to teach ACT3 principles.

 BREAK highlights a recess to provide personal time for restroom needs, informal conversations, and refreshments.

 PRAYER TIME highlights opportunities to break into pairs or triplets for specific points of prayer and establish a framework for ongoing prayer.

 HOMEWORK highlights the steps that require your prayerful reflection and completion between meetings. Assessments, worksheets, and *Calling Star* development are crucial to the discovery process.

 GOING DEEPER highlights the material that we believe to be very helpful in the discovery process, but which can't be covered within the time constraints of our meeting times.

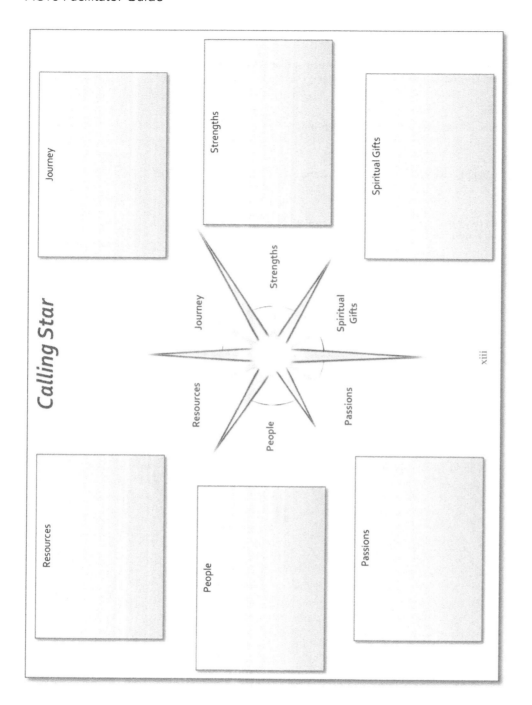

Calling Star

Journey

Strengths

Spiritual Gifts

Resources

People

Passions

xiii

ACT3 Participant Guide

Week 1 at a Glance
ReFocusing Your Heart

OUTCOMES

- Generate the tone for the interpersonal environment of the group with the personal introductions.
- Provide an overview of the *Calling Star* and establish its vital role in the Discovery process.
- Share Ephesians 1:15-19 as the Biblical basis for the certainty we have in God and His plan for our life.
- Create the expectation for the participant's completion of weekly homework assignments.

AGENDA

WELCOME AND OPENING PRAYER		
Welcome	• Team members • Commitment to timeliness • Stress the value of peer relationships	**Time:** 10 minutes
Personal Introductions	• First half of group sharing personal information	**Time:** 10 minutes
Guidance for a New Journey	• Commitment of the ACT3 Team	**Time:** 5 minutes
Introduction to Your *Calling Star*	• Brief overview of all six points of the star • Personal story of brightest point	**Time:** 30 minutes
BREAK		**Time: 15 minutes**
Personal Introductions	• Second half of group sharing personal information	**Time:** 10 minutes
Journey	• Journey Map • Show examples • Describe construction process	**Time:** 15 minutes
Ephesians 1:15-19	• Knowing God better	**Time:** 10 minutes
Three Powerful Impressions	• Hope of your calling • Your value in God's eyes • Incomparably great power	**Time:** 15 minutes
Praying Together	• Ephesians 1:17-19 prayer	**Time:** 5 minutes
Homework	• Praying for Ephesians 1 for peers • Complete Journey Map • Personality and Talents Assessment • Spiritual Gifts Assessment	**Time:** 5 minutes

Week 1: ReFocusing Your Heart

OPENING PRAYER

WELCOME TO ACT3

PERSONAL INTRODUCTIONS (ROUND I)

Welcome to Week ONE of ACT3! We are so excited to embark on this exciting journey TOGETHER! To get started, please share your name, a little bit about your family, your work/career, and the earliest memory you have of a spiritual moment that impacted your life.

GUIDANCE FOR A NEW JOURNEY
You're not the first to look to heaven for your next step

You are faced with countless choices and decisions every day. Some are easy—others are complex. As a 3rd Stager, you are in a new season of making life-directing decisions. To help you through this transformational process, you need the right information, practical tools, and strong support to gain clarity and execute what God has in store for you. That's why ACT3 exists. We do not want you to be surprised or anxious about change. Instead, we want to serve as a mentor and advocate on your behalf. The heart of our mission is to give you a clarifying confidence of your divine calling and a pathway to connect that calling to meaningful opportunities to serve.

15

WELCOME TO ACT3

	10 Min	Start Time: End Time:

- Begin this segment as soon as people are comfortable and ready to begin

- Facilitator introduces team members with host/hostess being introduced last on the list. Start every meeting with a reminder of the ACT3 purpose: *Connecting 3rd Stagers to people and opportunities to serve in alignment with their calling.*

- Host gives the welcome and any housekeeping details.

- Thank all your Discovery Growth Group Participants for making every effort to be present on time with the encouragement to come 10-15 minutes early to get settled and relaxed. This helps keep our commitment to being finished on time, which includes breaks.

- Life happens and unplanned emergencies arise. Emphasize that we fully understand and will support Discovery Growth Group Members when challenges occur, which can interrupt their plans. Outside of emergencies, thank them for committing to seven consecutive evenings. It will not only serve each person best, but it is crucial to the core value of developing peer relationships within the entire group.

- Invite them to use the Participants Guide to the fullest, taking notes and asking questions. It is made available for their benefit!

- Stress the importance of the relationships that will be forged within the group and the prime opportunity for the interaction and discovery of those next steps as a 3rd Stager. Most importantly, emphasize the value of **relaxing** and **engaging** during the next seven weeks!

- Explain the Discovery Group Roster. This is for sharing information amongst ourselves, jotting down information each week about your fellow cohorts. This will help you get to know each other and build relationships as we engage.

PERSONAL INTRODUCTIONS (ROUND I)

| 10 Min | Start Time: End Time: |

Teaching Points:

- Welcome everyone and introduce yourself first.

- Ask each participant to share their name, a snapshot of their family, work/career notes, and what they are expecting to gain from their Discovery experience. (This is a slight change from the questions in the Participant Guide.)

- **Note**: A total of 20 minutes between Round 1 and 2 means no more than 2 minutes per person.

Facilitator Tip:

- Take notes! Refer back to these stories as get-to-know data points.

GUIDANCE FOR A NEW JOURNEY

| 5 Min | Start Time: End Time: |

BIG IDEA

The natural cycles of life periodically bring us back to major decision points. The transitional steps from 2nd stage responsibilities to 3rd stage options have decisive impact on our life trajectory and outcome.

19

DESIRED OUTCOME

- To commit the ACT3 Team and all of our resources to help participants navigate these transitions and chart their course heading into, and living out, this promising 3rd stage of life.

- To raise the value and expectations of our Discovery process and to challenge participants to fully commit to the process with prayerful reflection and completion of every assessment and exercise.

Teaching Points:

- Describing the 3rd Stage is an early and critical juncture on the Discovery journey. Some will already be wondering if they are a 3rd Stager. It is mission critical that you define it as a *stage*, not an *age*. It is not confined to retirement. Retirement does markedly increase discretionary time, but it starts earlier.

- Consider using the following graph that depicts the relationship between discretionary time and available energy to describe the 3rd Stage.

- The 3rd Stage is marked by *increasing* discretionary time and *sufficient* available energy. It is our choice what we do with that time and energy. We want to help you make an informed choice.

- Neither accumulates, and both have plenty of options.

- There is no shortage of people in the 3rd Stage who claim they are busier than ever. The difference between the 2nd and 3rd Stages is that 3rd Stagers have the power of choice. As with our 401Ks and general finances, we may need some guidance as to how we allocate and manage our growing discretionary time.

- ACT3 defines the 3rd Stage as the **Investing Years**. The potential of the 3rd Stage is about **investing** what we were able to build in the 2nd Stage, with the intent of adding value to designated people, as well as making a difference in the world's issues around us.

THE FOUR STAGES OF LIFE AS A RELATIONSHIP BETWEEN DISCRETIONARY TIME AND AVAILABLE ENERGY

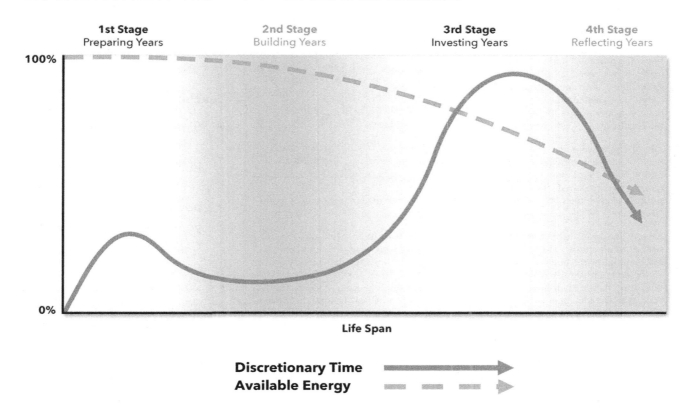

Personal Notes:

ACT3 Participant Guide

INTRODUCTION TO YOUR *CALLING STAR*
Know where you are headed

The adventurous, daring, and brave have always relied on a guide. Before GPS, maps, and compasses, travelers found stars that could point the way — none worthier and more admired than the North Star.

> *"Calling is the spur that keeps us journeying purposefully – and thus growing and maturing – to the very end of our lives."*
>
> Os Guinness, English author and social critic

The disciples were at a loss as to how they would get to where Jesus was calling them to go after He was resurrected. He reassured them with the promise to give them His Guide — the Holy Spirit — to help them navigate their assigned course.

Among the beautiful stories of the Advent is that of the Wise Men and the most famous of all stars — "His Star" as they called it. There were probably countless stars out that night stretching over a moonlit sky, but one Guiding Star shone brightly over all the others to signify that the world had changed in a moment. This Star led these guys from their distant home to the front door of the King they sought to worship — a child still no older than a toddler and completely dependent on His parents, Joseph and Mary. They were looking for the proverbial needle in a haystack, but the Star gave them directions to their destination. And at His feet they offered their worship — the gifts Father God provided in advance to meet the needs of Jesus' family during a difficult time.

As the disciples and Wise Men required a guiding star to lead them to their calling, so do we! ACT3 uses a unique tool entitled *Calling Star* to help you identify the key considerations in your search to find opportunities to serve in alignment with your calling. Your *Calling Star* is a composite picture of six distinct, yet related personal attributes that give insight to how God has wired you, where you have been, and where He wants to take you in order to fulfill His purpose for your life.

16

INTRODUCTION TO YOUR *CALLING STAR*

30 Min	Start Time:	
	End Time:	

Teaching Points:

- 5 minutes for introduction.

- Pull out personal loose version provided in participant's additional material folder or your own example of the *Calling Star*.

- 25 minutes includes covering all points of the *Calling Star* and brief personal stories for each point. These are not deep discussions – they are merely teasers.

- Cover each point at a high level and emphasize how it plays a role in how we were designed to follow our calling.

CALLING STAR

Resources   Journey

People   Strengths

Passions   Spiritual Gifts

JOURNEY: The story of your significant life events and experiences

STRENGTHS: Your natural talents (abilities, behaviors, and ways of thinking) with which you were born

SPIRITUAL GIFTS: "Others-focused" talents given by the Holy Spirit upon accepting Christ

PASSIONS: The good things that make your heart sing and the bad things that break your heart

PEOPLE: Those who have spoken into your life and those who are speaking into your life now

RESOURCES: Time (the 168 hours available to you each week and how you use them) and Skills (the abilities you've honed to do something well)

17

ACT3 Participant Guide

Each week of study within your ACT3 Discovery Growth Group is designed to help you dive deeper into these six points of your *Calling Star* and explore them both individually and collectively. We believe the Holy Spirit will enlighten you as you reflect on each point in a way that perhaps you have never considered before.

JOURNEY: *The story of your significant life events and experiences.*

What Paul wrote to the believers in Rome in Romans 8:28 was meant as more than reassurance that the frustrating circumstances in their lives would finally work out in the end. The key word is *everything*—God causes *everything* to work together for the good of those who love God and are called according to His purpose for them. You are no exception. The **Journey** point of your *Calling Star* comes into focus as you follow the outlined steps in the **Map Your Journey** (p. 25) exercise that we will discuss soon. Here you will spend time reflecting on how God has used your experiences to shape your life, led you to where you are, and prepared you for His climactic purpose for the rest of your life.

STRENGTHS: *Your natural talents (abilities, behaviors, and ways of thinking) with which you were born.*

David, the Psalmist, declared that God had created his inmost being—that God had knit him together in his mother's womb. David praised God because, as his Creator, He had made him wonderfully complex and that His workmanship was marvelous. Again, you are no exception. God wove your personality and natural talents into your DNA long before you prayed to receive new life in Christ. Your strengths and talents determine how you will go about doing what He has purposed to do through you. The **Strengths** point of your *Calling Star* comes into focus through the personal strengths assessment that will help you discover and understand your natural strengths and talents.

SPIRITUAL GIFTS: "*Others-focused*" talents given by the Holy Spirit upon accepting Christ.

Natural strengths and talents are given before your first breath, but spiritual gifts are not given until after a person asks in faith for new life from Jesus Christ. Those gifts are given to a confessing believer because of what He has purposed to do through that person. Paul says that you are no exception—spiritual gifts are given to each of us so we can help each other. The **Spiritual Gifts** point of your *Calling Star* comes into focus through a spiritual gifts assessment that will allow you to discover or reaffirm the gifts the Holy Spirit has given to you.

18

JOURNEY: *THE STORY OF YOUR SIGNIFICANT LIFE EVENTS AND EXPERIENCES*

Teaching Points:

- Describe the **Journey** point of the *Calling Star*.

- Events happen in your life and you may or may not know they are significant at the time.

My Story:

"*There have been a number of life events that have influenced me... the twists and turns and bends that have had the greatest impact in my life ... for example:*"

STRENGTHS: *YOUR NATURAL TALENTS (ABILITIES, BEHAVIORS, AND WAYS OF THINKING) WITH WHICH YOU WERE BORN*

Teaching Points:

- Describe the **Strengths** point of the *Calling Star*.

My Story:

Describe ways that you've used your personality. Tell the earliest story you can think of and how/where it happened.

SPIRITUAL GIFTS: *"OTHERS-FOCUSED"* TALENTS GIVEN BY THE HOLY SPIRIT UPON ACCEPTING CHRIST

Teaching Points:

- Describe the **Spiritual Gifts** point of the *Calling Star*.

- "Others-focused" talents given by the Holy Spirit upon accepting Christ.

- The gifts you are given are directly linked to the work God has planned for you.

My Story:

Describe a memorable way in which He used your gift(s) and ideally relate it to your **Strengths***. Describe the interaction between the two.*

PASSIONS: *The good things that make your heart sing and the bad things that break your heart.*

Passions — fires in the belly — are built as we get exposed to the realities of our world. There are good things in our world for which we are driven to protect and promote. And there are harmful things in our world, which we cannot tolerate or allow to go unchecked. The disciples recognized the presence and power of a personal passion in Jesus when He saw the abuses that were taking place in the Temple. They saw that it was eating Him alive. Jesus couldn't stand the thought that His Father's house was less than God intended. He couldn't live with those abuses He witnessed which dishonored His Father and hurt people. You are no exception in the capacity to "burn with a passion" deep inside of you. The **Passions** point of your *Calling Star* comes into focus as you work through a set of questions designed to challenge your thinking and to help you discover what makes, and what breaks, your heart.

PEOPLE: *Those who have spoken into your life and those who are speaking into your life now.*

We need more than traveling companions. We need trusted people God can use to speak into our lives. Jesus convinced Saul of Tarsus that he was way off course in life. Jesus chose a person named Ananias to help him see his next steps at this critical point in his journey. There is always a human component in God's system of giving His servants insight into their journey. You are no exception. The **People** point of your *Calling Star* comes into focus as you reflect on those people whom God has used in your life — past and present — and as we challenge you to open up to the possibility of adding to that list in the future.

RESOURCES: *A source of supply that can be drawn upon in order to achieve a desired outcome.*

Two resources that could particularly inform your place to serve are **Time** and **Skills**.

TIME: *The 168 hours available to you each week and how you use them.*

On day one of Creation, God created light and separated it from darkness. Though unstated, that one act also created time — the evening and the morning were the first day. After an unfathomable amount of creating on days two and three, God placed the sun, moon, and stars on the fourth day. The Bible clarifies that one of the purposes of those luminaries was to serve as signs to mark seasons and days and years. God meant for us to measure time and use it insightfully. Ecclesiastes teaches that there is a time for everything, and a season for every activity under heaven. You are no exception. The **Time** contribution to your *Calling Star* comes into focus as you

19

PASSIONS: *THE GOOD THINGS THAT MAKE YOUR HEART SING AND THE BAD THINGS THAT BREAK YOUR HEART*

Teaching Points:

- Describe the **Passions** point of the *Calling Star*.

- Our goal in ACT3 is to help you identify your passions or clarify them - not necessarily create them.

- What is the difference between what society says you should care about and what actually breaks your heart to the point that you're willing to do something about it? There are many worthy causes you can care about - some things on which you're willing to spend your money, and some things on which you're willing to spend your **Time**.

- It's OK to feel differently than your neighbor or spouse or friend - otherwise, everyone's passion would be the same! God is the one who lights your fire, and you will recognize it when He does.

- Part of the point of your *Calling Star* is to match how God made you with the passions He stirred in you, so that you can **do** something about it.

My Story:

Personal example…

PEOPLE: *THOSE WHO HAVE SPOKEN INTO YOUR LIFE AND THOSE WHO ARE SPEAKING INTO YOUR LIFE NOW*

Teaching Points:

- Describe the **People** point of the *Calling Star*.

- Prepare them to think about the life-shaping things that those special people said to them.

- Prepare them to think about who those people are that God can still use to speak to them.

My Story:

Personal example...
Idea: Reflect on your past teachers. Whose name can you remember? What about past bosses? Of these, which ones influenced your life in such a way that you not only remember their name, but also what they said to you?

RESOURCES: *A SOURCE OF SUPPLY THAT CAN BE DRAWN UPON IN ORDER TO ACHIEVE A DESIRED OUTCOME*

Teaching Points:

- Describe the **Time** contribution to the **Resources** point of your *Calling Star*.

- What changed when you became a 3rd Stager? Did you think you would have a lot of time, only to find out that you **don't**?

ACT3 Participant Guide

examine how you currently allocate your time and consider the possible redistribution of your time for the future.

SKILLS: *The ability to do something well; expertise.*

Skills are distinct from **Strengths** and **Spiritual Gifts**, yet they are still beautiful expressions of God's handiwork in your life. David was uniquely skilled as a musician, as well as a warrior. Exodus 31 tells of two men so gifted with craftsmanship that God personally chose them to build His Tabernacle for wilderness worship and the furniture that was made in the pattern of real objects in the Throne Room of Heaven. The **Skills** contribution to your *Calling Star* comes into focus as you identify the skills you have developed over time.

 BREAK

 PERSONAL INTRODUCTIONS (ROUND II)

Let's continue learning about one another. If you haven't already, please share your name, a little bit about your family, your work/career, and the earliest memory you have of a spiritual moment that impacted your life.

 **JOURNEY**
The story of your significant life events and experiences

Take a road trip down memory lane from the past to understand the present

Everyone has a story. Everyone has had experiences in their life—some good and some not so good—which helped shape them into the person they are today. You are no exception. Understanding who you are and how you came to be that way is one of the keys to successfully identifying where you can serve best. Many of the behaviors, preferences, and priorities you personally express in your life today are rooted in your past experiences, along with your response to them.

This insightful exercise asks you to examine some of these life lessons by creating a visual representation—an actual map—of your life journey.

20

Teaching Points

- Describe the **Skills** contribution to the **Resources** point of your *Calling Star*.

- How do your skillsets correlate to your passions?

- Sometimes **Skills** are formed at an early age in school or training. Sometimes they are formed throughout our career. Sometimes they form out of a hobby.

BREAK

⧗	**15 Min**	Start Time:
		End Time:

- Take a break, emphasize the need to come back on time to dive into Round II of Personal Introductions.

- Watch the time; if you need to make up to get back on schedule, you can shorten by at least 5 minutes.

- Be sure and give the partici-

pants a 5-minute notice to begin to regroup.

PERSONAL INTRODUCTIONS (ROUND II)

⧗	**10 Min**	Start Time:
		End Time:

- Continue introductions and take notes.

- Ask each participant to share their name, a snapshot of their family, work/career notes, and what they are expecting to gain from their Discovery experience. (This is a slight change from the questions in the Participant Guide.)

- **Note**: A total of 20 minutes between Round 1 and 2 means no more than 2 minutes per person.

JOURNEY

| 15 Min | Start Time:
End Time: |

The Bible has been described as God's Story. It certainly contains timelines of His work in Creation and with Mankind. It reveals who God is and His plans, as well as the big role players and major movements in His plan.

We have a story of our own. Mapping that story is a journey back through time that reminds us of the major people and big movements in our lives, how they connect, how they have shaped our lives, and how they inform our future. It becomes a revelation of God's presence and work in our lives.

DESIRED OUTCOME

- To excite participants to reflectively and prayerfully create their personal Journey Map by helping them to anticipate the key role it can play in the leading of the Holy Spirit to serving opportunities for which God has prepared in advance for them to do.

Teaching Points:

- Deeper overview of **Journey**. Why is it important? **Concept** teach.

- Note the Journey Worksheet on Page 25 in the Participant Guide.

- Show **list** of journey events. Emphasize **pray first**.

- Show Journey Map (the provided examples or your own map).

- Walk through the process. Emphasize that this is your **full** journey – even your life before knowing God, if that is the case.

- Facilitator shows their map: *"Allow yourself to be expressive. Like your life, your map will probably be filled with twists and turns. Use your imagination and don't be inhibited by thinking that your map needs to be linear, neat, or artistic."*

- This is not a biography you need to write. Pray about this so that when it goes on the page, you'll know what is significant and how they fit together.

- You will likely discover watershed events and turning point that shaped you, while maybe never having noticed them and their impact before.

EPHESIANS 1:15-19

⧖ 10 Min	Start Time:
	End Time:

Ephesians 1:15-19
For this reason, ever since I heard about your faith in the Lord Jesus and your love for all the saints, 16I have not stopped giving thanks for you, remembering you in my prayers. 17I keep asking that the God of our Lord Jesus Christ, the glorious Father, may give you the Spirit of wisdom and revelation, so that you may know Him better. 18I pray also that the eyes of your heart may be enlightened in order that you may know the hope to which He has called you, the riches of His glorious inheritance in the saints, 19and His incomparably great power for us who believe.

Our prayer for you is exactly Paul's prayer for his Ephesian friends—people just like you—people with a lasting faith, a passionate love for others, and a deep understanding of God's grace. Why? We are praying these four principles for you:

1. To know _____

Two primary Greek words are translated into English as "know." The first is a fact-based knowledge (I know your name). The second is the word that Paul uses because he wants to stress an intimate, experiential kind of knowledge (I am coming to know you). This "intimacy" requires more than just head knowledge; it requires a heart knowledge. It calls for an increasing awareness in hearing His voice more clearly and learning how to distinguish it, even when many others are speaking. Paul says this personal understanding of God and His presence will happen as God gives you the Spirit of wisdom and revelation.

FINDING YOUR "AHA!"
Discovering and discerning those God moments that breathe new life into your journey

To this growing knowledge of God is added a powerful trilogy of life changing "AHA!" moments. Paul was certainly no stranger to unexpected, inspirational, and yes, sometimes-painful insights that completely dismantled what he knew and took him in a different direction. The dramatic conversion of Saul of Tarsus to Paul the Apostle was the first of many that would alter his course, allowing him to encounter countless "light bulb" moments. This lifetime of connecting-the-dots paved the way for Paul to walk through the door of hope and unlock many learning experiences to know God on a much more intimate level.

☀ THE APERTURE OF THE HEART
Finding your Kodak Moment

Paul prays for the "eyes" to be enlightened for those who have experienced Jesus. In

21

The Ephesians 1 prayer is the foundational passage of the Discovery process that outlines the growing relationship and active partnership God wants with 3rd Stagers. The answer to this prayer opens every door and solidifies every hope we have for a meaningful and dynamic future.

- To make this prayer a foundational prayer for the rest of their life as they pursue God's plans for their own life, as well as the lives of those they love.

- To convince people that knowing God better is both possible and key to building the intimacy that is necessary to recognize His voice and to gain the trust that is necessary to do what He says.

Teaching Points:

- Facilitator reads passage.

- After reading, ask the entire group to circle the words "know" and "heart" in the verses.

- Share Paul's choice of the two options for the Greek words **know**:

  o One option is a type of "head knowledge" of facts. For instance, *I know your name*.

  o The option Paul used is a type of "heart knowledge" – it is a word that implies intimacy. That is, *I know you*.

- Share the importance of the use of the word **heart**. To the Greeks, it was the place where considerations are weighed and decisions are made.

- Paul knew that it was crucial to have an intimate knowledge of God when making decisions of the heart.

- There are four principles we want you to know...

1. TO KNOW GOD BETTER

BIG IDEA

God wants to be known better than we know Him. From the youngest in the room, to the eldest; from the least spiritually aware to the most spiritually mature, you can know God better. The more intimately we know God, the more certainly we can know our calling, our value, and His power.

DESIRED OUTCOME

- To encourage participants that their best days in their relationship with God are ahead of them.

- To challenge participants in potential thinking that aging is a guarantee of wisdom and increasing understanding of who God is and what God thinks. Wisdom is **not** natural. Revelation never runs out of insight. Both come **only** by the Spirit and both are **necessary** to know God intimately.

Teaching Points:

- Fill in the blank: To know <u>God better</u>.

- As believers, we yearn to grow in our walk with Christ. In fact, no one is ever excluded from this desire to know Him more deeply. How do we accomplish that, continually filling that void of wanting to be more like Christ and nourishing that deep desire to know Him better? Although helpful, it does not come from just a book, a class, or a teacher. The Holy Spirit is the source.

- Your best days of knowing God in deeper ways are still ahead of you. It makes no difference how long or short of time you've been walking with God, there are new insights God wants to give you as to who He is and what He wants to do.

- "Knowing God better" is pivotal to knowing your calling and finding your sweet spot in service. The better you know Him, the more easily and certainly you recognize His voice. Jesus said that His sheep hear His voice and follow Him. The better you know Him, the easier it is to trust Him when His call is to "get out of the boat" of your comfort zone and take the risks of obedience.

- **Question for Reflection:** Why is knowing God better so foundational to knowing your call and finding your service?

- o Answer: Jesus says in John 10 that we can recognize His voice: "My sheep hear my voice and follow."

- o Answer: When someone makes a big ask or leads us in a major decision, being able to trust them makes a huge difference in our willingness to say yes.

- o "Anything else?"

FINDING YOUR "AHA!"

Teaching Points:

- Introduce the concept of AHA! moments. This is when the lights come on and you get it!

  - o Share a very quick, personal example.

- Paul is the perfect example of an AHA! moment. He didn't know God as good as he thought he did until his dramatic conversion on the road to Damascus. When the lights came on, **everything changed** and he never forgot it.

- Encourage them that when it comes to God and spiritual truths, they can "get it!" God gave them the capacity to get it and the Holy Spirit is the Teacher to teach it.

THE APERTURE OF THE HEART

⏳ **5 Min**	Start Time: End Time:

BIG IDEA

Like the power of a photo from the past, the lasting effect of the Light of Heaven leaving an impression on the soul powerfully keeps our focus and directs our steps, even in the midst of chaos and the allure of other voices.

DESIRED OUTCOME

- To confirm in participants their capacity to "get it" and to experience their personal AHA! from God.

- To encourage each participant to consciously decide to push the button to the aperture of their heart and declare their openness to God's plan for their life, and their desire for the Holy Spirit to reveal it.

Teaching Points:

- Take a few quick photos of the group with your smart phone. Use this as an illustration for Aperture. Remind them that every time you hit the button, the aperture opens and another memory is made.

- Remind them of the power of a photo. It can make us happy, sad, grateful, etc.

- **Question for Reflection**: How does this vision carry you through discouragement, confusion, toil, hardship, and hard work in your service or calling for Christ?

today's world, Paul might have used the term "aperture," describing the opening of light into a camera that is exposed to a film and burns an image into a picture on the soul. When a photographer wants to capture an image, he or she clicks the button that opens the shutter, allowing light through the aperture to leave an impression and create a photo—that "Kodak Moment."

Paul is praying that the aperture of your heart, the place the Bible describes as the seat of your emotions and the place decisions are made, would open up to the powerful light of heaven and burn an eternal picture into your heart that you will never forget. Why? So that the picture of God's purpose may lead YOU, rather than all of the distractions that work to control your life, sap your energy, and subvert God's plans.

2. To know _____

It has been said that the most important day of your life is the day you were born and that the second most important day is when you discover why. The answer to that question changes everything! How do you find out and unleash the WHY? The journey to answering this profound, life-altering question leads you to HOPE, which is fuel for your calling.

A calling from God is like a "summons of the soul" where He directs your attention to a place He wants you to be or a mission He assigns you to undertake. God created you to be unique! That is why He speaks specifically to you. However, there will be challenges. You may have doubts and fears about your strengths and weaknesses. But do not be discouraged—rather, be encouraged! God is giving you new insights and revelations. God is calling you. God is choosing you. God is commissioning you to step to a new cadence. Let's take a look at what the Scripture says:

- *…I have called him. I will bring him, and he will succeed in his mission. (Isa. 48:15)*

- *"For I know the plans I have for you," declares the Lord, "plans to prosper you and not to harm you, plans to give you hope and a future." (Jer. 29:11)*

- *I urge you to live a life worthy of the calling you have received. (Eph. 4:1)*

- *…For God's gifts and His call are irrevocable. (Rom. 11:29)*

3. To know _____

How do you know that you are valuable to God? For starters, it begins in the Manger at the joyful birth of a baby and continues with the revelation of God's love at the Cross. But it does not stop there. There are countless verses that demonstrate how God wonderfully sees you, such as:

22

2. TO KNOW THE HOPE OF YOUR CALLING

⏳ 5 Min	Start Time:
	End Time:

BIG IDEA

Confidence in your future flows from certainty of your calling.

DESIRED OUTCOME

- To convince people to pursue God's plan for their life.

Teaching Points:

- The first impression Paul prays that will be left on their soul was to know the hope of their calling (fill in <u>the hope of your calling</u>).

- There are multiple and powerful promises all throughout scripture teaching that God has a plan and a calling for your life.

- Read your personal favorite verse(s) provided in their notes on p. 22 of their Participant Guide.

- Give an example of "a summons of the soul."

  o A compelling whisper in the ear

  o Drafts during war times

  o Proposal of marriage

  o NFL Draft

- This passage teaches that God will speak to your soul about His plans for you.

3. TO KNOW <u>YOUR VALUE IN GOD'S EYES</u>

5 Min	Start Time:
	End Time:

BIG IDEA

One of the biggest questions of Creation is, *"So, what does God get out of this for all of His trouble?"* Wonder no more! When the dust of Creation finally settles and the last tick of time goes silent, God wants only **one** thing…**you**! You are **His** inheritance. He did all of this to end up with you! Line it all up and look it all over. God chooses you!

DESIRED OUTCOME

- To reassure the participants that this is not just some utilitarian relationship, as if *God needs you to do something for Him.* Absolutely not! God is going to keep doing what He has always, and will continue, to do. He just wants you to do it with Him in a meaningful way. He's like any parent loving to have his or her child at their side in the family business.

Teaching Points:

- The 2nd powerful picture Paul prays will be imprinted on their soul is their value in God's eyes (fill in your value).

- Reinforce the supporting scriptures of this point provided at the top of p. 23 of their Participant Guide. Read each one of them.

- The summation of this point is that God loves you.

- Ask the impact of knowing that God loves them on their response to God's call on their life and His leadership as to the specific tasks He has prepared for them to do.

- *You are God's workmanship – a masterpiece of His own hands. (Eph. 2:10)*

- *You are fearfully and wonderfully made. (Ps. 139:14)*

- *He chose you before the foundation of the world! (Eph. 1:11)*

- *We have different gifts, according to the grace given us. (Rom. 12:6)*

4. To know _____ **available to live out your calling**

This incomparably great power is best used to describe the most powerful event that has ever happened – the resurrection of Jesus Christ. Paul says this same mighty power that God exercised to raise Jesus from the dead is available to YOU. Yes, this life-changing power lives within you!

- You may feel that life is slipping you by and that your best "life-giving" days are over. But this incomparably great power exceeds the power of death in any of life's circumstances. Expect transformation and pursue spiritual growth. Your best days are ahead of you!

- You may feel that you have lost any position or platform to make a difference. But this incredibly great power not only raised Jesus from the dead, but "seated" Him in a position high enough to do exactly what the Father called Him to do. This same power can seat you – position you, exactly where God needs you to be, bringing clarity and purpose to your life!

- You may feel like all hell is breaking loose when the spirit of chaos and confusion challenges your every step. The enemy does not want you to fulfill your calling, much less hear the Voice of God. However, do not fear the enemy's deception, which causes confusion and doubt. This incomparably great power has already defeated Satan and every demon of Hell who collectively tried to stop Jesus. Rest assured, they couldn't stop Him – and that same Power will keep them from stopping you!

To sum it all up, as you continue to grow in your relationship with God and find your "next steps" of your calling and purpose, it is crucial that you intimately recognize four valuable lessons. You need to:

1. KNOW God better than you do right now

2. KNOW God's calling for you

3. KNOW the value God places on you

4. KNOW the power He has made available to you

23

4. TO KNOW <u>THE INCOMPARABLY GREAT POWER</u> AVAILABLE TO LIVE OUT YOUR CALLING

5 Min	Start Time: End Time:

Following Jesus and living life on point **is no walk in the park**. It is still not natural for us to live unselfishly. Even once we overcome our natural tendencies, what He asks us to do will have its challenges. But even if it were natural to us and was to do, we have an **enemy** intent on making life and obedience very hard. There will always be a wind in our face.

Jesus continues His responsibilities in Heaven. Father God positioned Him where nothing and no one could stop Him. He overcame Sin and Death. He overcame every demon of hell and every opposing human on earth. The same power that authorizes and empowers Jesus to hold Creation together and intercede on our behalf is the same power available to God's people to be raised out of the grip of death-wielding circumstances, and powerful opposition.

DESIRED OUTCOME

- To excite the participants with the possibility of living beyond themselves and their own limitations.

- To anticipate the sense of the soul that God is not only with them, but also working through them.

- To live with the confidence that they can live out their calling in a meaningful way, regardless of challenges of the past or the opposition in the present.

Teaching Points:

- Fill in <u>incomparably great power</u>.

- The 3rd powerful impression Paul wants left on their soul is that the exact same Spirit that entered the dead body of Jesus and raised Him from the dead will energize them to rise above all their own personal resistance and challenges. That power is not a dumbed down version, it is the **incomparably great power** available to live out your calling.

- Use personal example of a power boost.

- Can use the example of the Red Key to a Dodge Hellcat — which unlocks the engine and lets it go from 500 HP to 707 HP! He gives us the Red Key!

- The same mighty power that God put forth to raise Jesus is available to you.

ACT3 Participant Guide

PRAYING TOGETHER

Ephesians 1:17-19 *(paraphrased)*
God, I ask you to bless _____. I pray that you would give _____ the Spirit of wisdom and revelation, so that (he/she) may know You better. I pray also that the eyes of _____ heart may be enlightened in order that (he/she) may know the hope of (his/her) calling, and that (he/she) may know the value You place on (him/her), and that _____ may know Your incomparably great power at work in (him/her) as (he/she) believes. In Jesus name I pray. Amen!

HOMEWORK

- Pray Eph. 1:17-19 prayer (card provided) for each member of the Discovery Growth Group individually at some point through the coming week. Pray for two different people each day.

- Spend some time prayerfully reflecting on your life experiences and complete the **Journey Worksheet** (p. 25).

- If you have not already taken both the **Personal Strengths Assessment** (provided separately) and the **Spiritual Gifts Assessment** (p. 47), please do so before next week. (Instructions were provided in the welcome emails to you. If you cannot find these, please contact one of your facilitators).

CLOSING PRAYER

24

PRAYING TOGETHER

5 Min	Start Time:
	End Time:

Teaching Points:

- Remind the participants of the aperture illustration.

- Remind them of their part in saying yes to the Holy Spirit's work and opening up to whatever future God has for them.

- Then remind them of God's role in planning His purposes for them and providing the light to see it.

- Refer the participants to the Eph. 1:17-19 prayer printed on page 24.

- Instruct the participants to break up in pairs and pray Eph. 1:17-19 over each other.

- Demonstrate by one facilitator praying over the other facilitator.

- Encourage full participation, using the verses as the content of the prayer, adding in the name to make it personal.

Journey Worksheet

Understanding who you are and how you came to be that way is one of the keys to successfully identifying where you can best serve. Much of your behavior, preferences, and focus today are rooted in your past experiences and your response to them. Take some time to think back over the key experiences that shaped who you are as a person today. What were the major punctuation points, as well as the turning points?

Below are some ideas to consider:

- Major assignments, experiences, relationships, hardships, or personal changes

- Significant crossings where you made important choices

- Passages that led to new insights or learning

- 'Aha'! moments when God spoke directly to you

- Times when you found yourself feeling like you were at a stalling point

- Markers or mileposts, mountains or deserts, valleys, sharp turns, and/or islands

- Important people who joined you and/or left you along the way

Your assignment is to draw the map of your **Journey** in a way that tells the story of your life. Two examples have been provided for your reference, but remember, this is *your journey*, and it will be *your story*. It doesn't have to be pretty or perfectly organized; it just has to tell your story.

TIPS:

- *We suggest that you may want to start by making a list of the experiences in your life to organize your thoughts before drawing.*

- *You may want to consider your life in seasons or decades to help organize what you would like to highlight.*

- *Try to set aside time every day this week to work on your life journey map. Ask God to bring events and people back to your remembrance.*

- *Feel free to highlight, color, draw pictures, etc. as God reveals those significant "aha" moments you might have overlooked or forgotten.*

25

ACT3 Participant Guide

Next week we will spend time sharing the map of your **Journey** one-on-one.

JOURNEY WORKSHEET NOTES:

26

Week 2 at a Glance
ReThinking Your Path

OUTCOMES

- Develop an understanding that the best decisions are always preceded by best thinking.
- Solidify the value of life experiences through the peer sharing of their Journey Maps.
- Create an expectation that God has been actively involved in our past in preparation for our future.
- Establish Jesus as the model for serving.
- Raise the value of finished homework and a completed *Calling Star*.

AGENDA

WELCOME AND OPENING PRAYER		
Changing How You Think	• Romans 12:2 • The call to rethink	**Time:** 15 minutes
Group Discussion: What We Might Rethink		**Time: 10 minutes**
Personal Sharing: Your Journey Map		**Time: 45 minutes**
BREAK		**Time: 15 minutes**
Rethinking Your Past	• 1 Peter 1:1-2 • God has chosen you • You can feel out of place • You've been intentionally planted	**Time:** 10 minutes
Table Talk: What's the Greatest Opportunity Where You Are?		**Time: 10 minutes**
The Model for Rethinking	• Philippians 2:5-8 • Talk about Jesus • Setup for Going Deeper	**Time:** 10 minutes
Praying Together	• Philippians 2 prayer • Break into pairs	**Time:** 5 minutes
Homework	• Going Deeper on Philippians 2 • Complete **Journey** point of *Calling Star* • Complete Talents Assessment • Praying for Philippians 2:5-8 for peers	**Time:** 5 minutes

---

Week 2: ReThinking Your Path

OPENING PRAYER

FINDING YOUR WAY
It starts with how you think

We are living longer and healthier lives. According to experts, we can expect to live another 20-30 years of reasonable healthiness following retirement, especially due to advances in technology and improvements in healthier lifestyles. At the same time, 3rd Stagers are increasingly unwilling to drift into personal irrelevance. But how do you fight the strong currents of self-centeredness and the cultural mindset of leisurely pursuit that can sweep you exactly where you don't want to go?

> *"We cannot solve our problems with the same thinking we used to create them."*
>
> Albert Einstein

It all starts with how you think. It's pretty simple, really. If you want to be different, you have to think differently. Want to see a change? Change the way you think.

No person in history had to endure a more radical mindset change than Saul of Tarsus as he became the Apostle Paul. From being blinded by the Darkness to being blinded by the Light. From actively persecuting Christians to being persecuted and imprisoned himself. Changing from a zealot as a Roman citizen and Pharisee to being zealous for the souls of lost people. Converted from being an advocate of legalism to being a champion of grace. EVERYTHING CHANGED. No wonder the Holy Spirit used Paul to challenge the Christians at Rome to think differently. He had experienced the ultimate of mindset transformations.

27

Reminders:

- Start as close to the designated start time as possible. Thank them for timely starts, which lead to timely finishes.

- As you welcome, remind the group of our purpose: *To connect 3rd Stagers to people and opportunities to serve in alignment with their calling.*

- Thank them for making their homework a priority.

- Pray for the time together.

FINDING YOUR WAY

Teaching Tips

5 Min	Start Time: End Time:

- After reading, ask the entire group to circle the words "do" and "be" in the verse.

- Ask the participants how their parents communicated a cease-and-desist order as a child.

  o Example: When a mom sometimes tells a child, *"Don't even think about it!"*

- Whenever God says, *"Do not,"* there is **no** wiggle room.

- Whenever God says, *"Let there be…"* Genesis 1-2 demonstrates that while a lot of things happen.

- This cannot be clearer: *God is expecting us to see things His way*, not just because He deserves our respect, but because He knows that what we do starts with how we think.

- Since what we do starts with what we think, this passage is pivotal as an early step in the Discovery process and the final step in actually serving in alignment with your calling.

Personal Notes:

ACT3 Participant Guide

Romans 12:2
Do not conform any longer to the pattern of this world, but be transformed by the renewing of your mind. Then you will be able to test and approve what God's will is — His good, pleasing, and perfect will.

THE CALL TO RETHINK THE PATH FORWARD

There are no stronger commands from God than "Do not" and "Let there be." Therefore, when God says, "Do not be conformed" and "be transformed," you can rest assured that change is in the works.

The contemporary term for "pattern of this world" is _____.

Paul is most likely not thinking about big sin issues here, but rather those that are common sense, simple matters of obedience. He has their core values and priority list in mind — how they view their material possessions, their personal freedoms, and the needs of others.

Conformation is taking the shape of _____
and putting the squeeze on who you are at the very heart of what matters inside.

Conformation starts with external pressures, but eventually shapes what we think and do. In today's world, we hear the constant drumbeat of do your own thing…it's okay because everyone else — from the famous to your friends — is doing it. We constantly struggle with rationalizing our thoughts and actions. The effect is usually temporary, yet constantly taking on new shapes, because as soon as the pressure points change, like all trends or fashions do, how we think and what we do changes, too.

Transformation is an inside job that converts your _____ and

_____.

Transformation starts by changing how we think. Forgiveness and salvation start with a change of thinking on our part and are demonstrated in our confession and repentance. Transformation must start with confession of our wrong thinking and conformity in subtle ways to the "norms" of our world. Transformation must include repentance and a commitment to a new approach to living.

WHAT WE MIGHT RETHINK

28

THE CALL TO RETHINK THE PATH FORWARD

⧖ 10 Min	Start Time:
	End Time:

BIG IDEA

When our thinking conflicts with God's thinking and threatens His plans, He doesn't hesitate to demand that we rethink our position. The cultural norms for American 3rd Stager living; the reality of longer, healthier lives; and the inherent longing for personal fulfillment has created a conflict of the soul that can only be resolved by the Biblical mandate to rethink our approach to this new season of options.

DESIRED OUTCOME

- To challenge participants to evaluate the core values that influence the decisions they make regarding how they will live out the 3rd stage of their lives.

- To guide them towards alignment with Biblical principles when deciding.

- To encourage them to spend time beyond these 10 minutes in prayerful reflection with their heart open to the voice of the Holy Spirit.

Teaching Points:

- True transformation begins with thinking differently.

- *On 2nd thought…* That's the essence of what Paul is asking the Romans to do, and what we want our participants to do.

- No person in history was more directly confronted by God for His thinking and had a more profound transformation in thinking and doing than Paul. There could be no more fitting person to hold the pen and transcribe God's Word on this teaching than Paul.

- Fill in the 1st blank: <u>cultural norm</u>.

- Cultural norms are the standards we live by. They are the shared expectations and rules that guide behavior of people within social groups. Cultural norms are learned and reinforced from parents, friends, teachers, and others while growing up in a society.

- Fill in the 2nd blank: <u>outward pressures.</u>

- Fill in the 3rd blanks: <u>character</u> and <u>core values.</u>

WHAT WE MIGHT RETHINK

10 Min	Start Time: End Time:

Week 2: ReThinking Your Path

- What are the cultural norms for American 3rd Stagers? How do they differ inside the church?

- How might the Holy Spirit want us to ReTHINK these norms?

 **TABLE TALK**
The map of your Journey

Over the next 45 minutes or so, reflect on the following questions together as you share the map of your **Journey**:

- What did you learn, or confirm, about yourself by looking at your **Journey** in this way?

- What are three of the most impactful events of your life?

- How do those life-shaping events impact the way you live today? How might they impact your choices for the future?

- How can you see your **Journey** fitting into God's plan for you and His larger mission for the world?

BREAK

29

TABLE TALK

⧖ 45 Min	Start Time: End Time:

Teaching Points:

- We hope you really put some time and thought into the *My Journey Map* this past week! Your personal life map illustrates where you have been and where you have come from to arrive where you are **today**!

- We've all been there. Mountain peaks, low valleys, wildernesses, crossroads, back roads, gravel roads, forks in the road, rivers to traverse, bridges to cross, twists and turns around the bend, through the dense woods, trails with obstacles, paths of opportunities, difficult decisions to make, mistakes along the way, wisdom of the day, the highs and the lows, the cheers and the tears, and so much more. Understanding all the green, yellow, and red stop signs along the way not only gives you a more focused perspective of your past, but they project a realistic view of what to embrace or to avoid ahead on the road to finding God's new calling for you.

- Take about 45 minutes, partner with someone in the group to share your journey, and discuss the questions listed here.

- Once you're finished discussing, we will go directly into a break.

- Instruct the pairs that the Break follows the 45 minutes of sharing. Invite them to break when finished, with the flexibility of going to break early, or using some of the break time for additional sharing.

- Give notice to the pairs at the mid-point to help insure time for mutual sharing.

BREAK

15 Min	Start Time: End Time:

ACT3 Participant Guide

1 Peter 1:1-2
Peter, an apostle of Jesus Christ, to God's elect, strangers in the world, scattered throughout Pontus, Galatia, Cappadocia, Asia and Bithynia, ²who have been chosen according to the foreknowledge of God the Father, through the sanctifying work of the Spirit, for obedience to Jesus Christ and sprinkling by His blood.

THE NEED TO RETHINK THE PATH YOU'VE WALKED

Shifting family dynamics; considering, entering, or enjoying a form of retirement; an evolving social world—these are all markers of 3rd Stagers. If only one word were used to describe the 3rd stage of life, it would have to be *transition*. It is that stage of life that often brings unwelcomed monumental change and a tsunami of feelings and emotions. Transition exposes us to the soul-jarring questions of "Who am I now? How did I get here? Why am I here?" Are you prepared for the answers?

In the Scripture above, Peter comes alongside a group of disoriented believers to help them regain their bearings. They had not braced themselves for the realities of their displacement from the familiar, and they were a little dazed by their "new normal." With the first strokes of the pen in his first letter, Peter stabilizes his friends' thinking by challenging them to rethink their answers to the same haunting questions we find ourselves asking: How did I get here and where is God in this?

Even though you may have doubts, God has _____.

To be chosen by God involves thoughtful and deliberate consideration by Him, in the spirit of His kindness, favor, mercy, and love. God not only has a plan for the world, He has a plan just for YOU. He has a mission with your name on it to help carry out His plan. You just need to answer the call.

The transitions of life can make you feel _____.

The people and culture that Peter addresses are the exact same ones that give rise to Fiddler on the Roof and its iconic song: Tradition! Papa, mama, sons, and daughters know their verses, as well as the tune. What's more, after centuries of exile, Jews find ways to get back to their promised land. No small part of their identity is their homeland.

When Peter calls these God-chosen people *strangers*, he is hits a raw nerve and undoubtedly causes personal pain. It is a powerful word for Peter to use to describe these believers. It emphasizes a transitional state. Peter's choice of the word acknowledges that their feet are not standing where their roots are firmly planted and their current home is not where their heart is.

The original Greek word describes a resident-foreigner. For some in today's world,

30

THE NEED TO RETHINK THE PATH YOU'VE WALKED

⏳ 20 Min	Start Time:
	End Time:

Teaching Points:

- After reading, ask the entire group to circle the words "elect" and "chosen" in the verses below. Put a box around "strangers" and underline "scattered."

- There has never been a time in history where there are more "out-of-place" people in the world. World Vision says nearly 1 out of every 100 people on the planet is displaced (65 million people).

Even though you may have doubts, God has <u>chosen you</u>.

Teaching Points:

- Fill in the blank: <u>chosen you</u>.

- Whether as a 3rd Stager in general, or as an individual specifically, we can feel like we have become the "un-chosen" or "overlooked."

The transitions of life can make you feel <u>out of place</u>.

Teaching Points:

- Fill in the blank: <u>out of place</u>.

- Point out the issues of being a contemporary alien or refugee: Dress code, diet, language, mannerisms, religion, and different worship styles.

- Think about a time when you travelled out of the country, or gathered in a new group where it felt like all the others knew each other but you.

Personal Notes:

traveling or moving to a different country is an exciting adventure. For others, it can feel unfamiliar, awkward, and even stressful just walking down the street or getting in a taxi. This word describes someone, not simply traveling, but living in a foreign culture—like that proverbial "fish out of water" feeling when faced with new smells, sounds, textures, faces, places, and mores.

You have not been randomly tossed into life, but rather God has

_____.

Don't miss Peter's choice to use the word *scattered*. At first glance to us, this well-known farming term in biblical days may sound like a discombobulated flinging of seed. Oh my, you would be overlooking one of the powerful messages Peter wanted these struggling believers to get!

Remember that Peter was addressing people living in an agrarian culture. With wide-eyed wonder, they would have read that word we have translated into English as *scattered*. In actuality, it is a perfect choice of words, if you want to convey a sense of intentionality and strategy.

For example, a Midwest grain farmer plants 200 million corn and bean seeds every spring. When using the latest technology described as prescription farming, the farmer knows everything required to make an informed decision as to the planting of each seed. He knows the genetics of the seed, exactly where the seed is being planted in the field, the soil type in that part of the field, the optimum spacing between each seed in that particular soil, and the exact depth the seed should be planted for the weather conditions. Why? For maximum production in his fields come harvest time.

God is looking at the end of our life from the very beginning, our personal planting, if you will. He knows where He wants you, how to get you there, and how to use you right where you are today!

These believers are many miles from their ancestral homeland. They obviously felt uncomfortable where they were living. They likely were worried about the impact it would have on their children and on future generations. With this familiar term, Peter changes their perspective and raises their hopes. He tells them they have been intentionally planted exactly where God had intended them to be all the time! They can be blessed and have eternal impact, where they are.

TABLE TALK

- In what areas, if any, are you feeling like a stranger—out of place—at this point in your life?

31

You have not been randomly tossed into life, but rather God has <u>intentionally planted you</u>.

Teaching Points:

- Fill in the blank: <u>intentionally planted you</u>.

BIG IDEA

The circumstances and experiences of life can cause confusion and uncertainty for 3rd Stagers about their future. God is a mind reader! He pays close attention to what we think about His commitment to us, our relationships with the people around us, and how our past prepares us for our future.

God is not stuck with you, nor does He just let you wander into your future. God has been actively involved in your past as He prepares you for your future.

DESIRED OUTCOME

- To challenge participants to prepare their minds for action as they navigate the transition of life and rest in His love for them and His preparations for their future.

- To encourage people that they have been chosen, prepared, and placed by God in alignment with His purposes for their life. He will not waste His investment in your life or a crisis you've endured.

- To raise their expectations that what God has planned for them is close to where they are or in a place that He will lead them to go.

Personal Notes:

TABLE TALK

⧖	**10 Min**	Start Time: End Time:

- Do you believe that God has chosen you and planted you where you are? Are there any ways it surprises you that God has planted you where you are? If so, what might be the strategic advantage to God of planting you there?

Philippians 2:5-8
Let this mind be in you which was also in Christ Jesus, ⁶who, being in the form of God, did not consider it robbery to be equal with God, ⁷but made Himself of no reputation, taking the form of a bondservant, and coming in the likeness of men. ⁸And being found in appearance as a man, He humbled Himself and became obedient to the point of death, even the death of the cross. (NKJV)

The perfect model for ReThinking is Jesus. No one has ever more perfectly followed through with the plans of Father God. No one has ever had to adjust more to the reality of changing circumstances in order to complete His assignment. And no one has ever had such impact on the world because of the adjustments so willingly made.

The watershed mindset of Jesus, and His humble obedience deserves a deeper dive on your part. We will help you go there by spending time in the GOING DEEPER section at the end of this session.

This challenge is no easy feat. But Paul understood the need for a reset of our thinking. And Paul wanted his dear friends to experience the fullest potential of their lives. This passage is not just the setting of a standard; it can become the powerful cry of your heart, both for yourself, as well as the people in your life.

 **PRAYING TOGETHER**

Phil 2:5-8 (paraphrased)
Father God, I pray that You will help _____ to have the same mind – the same kind of thinking – which was also in Christ Jesus, who, being in the form of God, did not consider it robbery to be equal with God. Like you did, Jesus, help _____ to make himself/herself of no reputation. Help him/her to take on the form of a bondservant. Now, as a bondservant, I pray that you will help him/her to be humble and live obediently to YOUR revealed will to his/her last breath. In Jesus name, Amen!

PHILIPPIANS 2:5-8

⏳ 10 Min	Start Time: End Time:

Teaching Points:

- This challenge is no easy feat. But Paul understood the need for a reset of our thinking. And Paul wanted his dear friends to experience the fullest potential of their lives. This passage is not just the setting of a standard; it can become the powerful cry of our heart.

- Prepare the participants for a deeper diver for personal benefit through further study next week.

PRAYING TOGETHER

⏳ 5 Min	Start Time: End Time:

Teaching Points:

- Lead the participants in an exercise that uses this passage as a pattern for prayer. Choose either your co-facilitator, or your home host and pray for them to demonstrate the use of this prayer.

- Ask them to break into pairs and pray Philippians 2:5-8 over each other.

HOMEWORK

- During your quiet time this week, use the Going Deeper Guide at the end of this session to reflect on Philippians 2:5-8 and ask the Holy Spirit to help you think about Jesus as a model for ReTHINKING.

- Spend some time prayerfully reflecting on the map of your **Journey** (p. 25). Ask the Holy Spirit to identify the most significant 2-3 life events, experiences, or "aha" moments that He has used to get you to where you are, as well as shape who you are and how you think. Write these 2-3 experiences in the **Journey** point of your *Calling Star* (p. xiii).

- Prayerfully study the results of your strengths assessment (provided separately) and bring them with you next week.

- Use the provided card to pray the Philippians 2:5-8 prayer for each member of the Discovery Growth Group individually at some point through the coming week. Pray for two different people each day.

CLOSING PRAYER

 GOING DEEPER

 Philippians 2:5-8
Let this mind be in you which was also in Christ Jesus, ⁶who, being in the form of God, did not consider it robbery to be equal with God, ⁷but made Himself of no reputation, taking the form of a bondservant, and coming in the likeness of men. ⁸And being found in appearance as a man, He humbled Himself and became obedient to the point of death, even the death of the cross. (NKJV)

3rd Stager believers find themselves in a distinct dilemma: The 3rd Stage of life is the most culturally acceptable time to live in a self-centered way. In this context, no fight is bigger for American 3rd Stagers than a sense of entitlement. "We earned it and the world owes us."

However, the pathway to making life count is paved with sacrifice. We need a champion to show us the pathway to servanthood. Paul tells us to look no farther than Jesus. He is the model of ReThinking! Philippians 2:5-8 sums up the response of Jesus

33

ACT3 Participant Guide

to His Father when asked to assume the most demanding assignment ever delegated.

From this passage (and other scriptures), how was the life of Jesus different for Him as a man on earth, as compared to His life as the Son of God in heaven?

- What were His prerogatives?
  - In Heaven?

  - On Earth?

- What were His limitations?
  - In Heaven?

  - On Earth?

- What was His status among those around Him?
  - In Heaven?

  - On Earth?

Note the differences. Paul wanted us to know that Jesus made a strategic decision to put Himself in the vulnerable position of Manhood. Circle the words in this passage that were personal choices on His part in order to fulfill His calling.

Reflect on the status and rights you earned in the 2nd stage of life and the benefits you have understandably anticipated as a 3rd Stager. If we ReTHINK our prerogatives as 3rd Stagers, what strategic decisions might you have to make in order to live out God's purpose for you?

34

Week 3 at a Glance
ReDiscovering Your Strengths

OUTCOMES

- Develop an understanding that the participant is *uniquely them* by design of the Master and that it is a lifelong process which starts early and leverages all of life's experiences.
- Develop an understanding of natural talents and personality traits and how God uses us by using them.
- Solidify their understanding of their natural talents and traits and an anticipation for God using them.
- Create the potential for out-of-the-box thoughts inspired by God.
- Continue to raise the value of finished homework and a completed *Calling Star*.

AGENDA

WELCOME AND OPENING PRAYER		
The Master's Masterpiece	• Ephesians 2:10 • The Master holds the brush	**Time:** 5 minutes
The First Stroke of the Brush	• Psalms 139:13-14 • The DNA stroke of the masterpiece	**Time:** 5 minutes
Introduction to Natural Talents and Personality Traits	• Uniquely you before you were born • General observations • Discretionary examples • Summary principles of natural talents and personality traits	**Time:** 35 minutes
BREAK (Can mix and match with personal sharing time)		**Time: 15 minutes**
Personal Sharing of Assessment	• Which of your talents is your favorite? • When have you seen God use that talent? • Which talent is most edgy? • Which talent do you wish you had more of?	**Time:** 40 minutes
Dreaming Out of the Box	• Acts 2:17 • Counterintuitively, 3rd Stagers seem to be God's choice to be the dreamers! • Use this portion if possible. But if time is short, it can be relegated to deeper thinking with a quick overview. It is a key point to ACT3, but it can carry itself.	**Time:** 10 minutes
Table Talk: Sharing of personal out-of-the-box thinking for ministries		**Time: 10 minutes**
Praying Together	• Exchange nametags • Pray for renewal, insights, opportunities	**Time:** 5 minutes

Homework	• Pray daily for person of nametag • Complete Strengths Worksheet • Transfer findings to your *Calling Star* • Reflect on findings and Journey Map • Complete Spiritual Gifts Assessment	**Time:** 5 minutes

Reminders:

- Start as close to the designated start time as possible with Ephesians 2:10.

- Move to Ephesians 2:10 as quickly as possible.

- As you welcome, remind the group of our purpose: *To connect 3rd Stagers to people and opportunities to serve in alignment with their calling.*

Week 3: ReDiscovering Your Strengths

OPENING PRAYER

STRENGTHS
Your natural talents (abilities, behaviors, and ways of thinking) with which you were born

Ephesians 2:10
For we are God's workmanship, created in Christ Jesus to do good works, which God prepared in advance for us to do.

At heart, artists want credit for their work. Painters leave their inscription. Potters leave their stamp. We should not be surprised to learn that the Great Artist leaves His Seal.

Like a master painter with all the colors of the palate and the tools of the trade at the artist's disposal, God has limitless options available to make us each uniquely beautiful and useful. The choices are His. Each stroke of the brush, every turn of the wheel, and every cut of the chisel is His to make. Out of all you could be, He created you intentionally to be who you are in Christ. He had purposes in mind when He did.

And the Great Artist's first act in creating you was early.

Psalms 139:13-14
For You created my inmost being; You knit me together in my mother's womb. [14]I praise You because I am fearfully and wonderfully made.

35

STRENGTHS & EPHESIANS 2:10

5 Min	Start Time:
	End Time:

BIG IDEA

A masterpiece is created according to the vision and expertise of the Master over time. The masterpiece is a reflection of the greatness (glory) of the master. It usually is meant to serve a specific purpose the artist had in mind. And it serves as a source of admiration and enjoyment to the observers. As the Master's masterpiece, we fulfill all three roles.

- To encourage participants that they are a life-long work of the Father and to anticipate His ongoing work in their lives.

- To settle that they have been created with a designed purpose in mind and to stir a deep sense of curiosity as to what that purpose might be.

Teaching Points:

- As the prayer of Ephesians 1 is the heart of the ACT3 Discovery process, Ephesians 2:10 is its foundation. The twin pillars of personal worth and individual purpose rest firmly on the declaration that we are each the Master's masterpiece and that He created us with our purpose in mind.

- In Ephesians 3, Paul then declares that redeemed and purpose-fulfilling people are an indisputable and eternal demonstration of His glory.

PSALMS 139:13-14

| 5 Min | Start Time: End Time: |

Teaching Points:

- Geneticists are awed at this early reference of the role DNA and the governing impact that it has on the human personality and physical makeup.

- The Master holds the brush and it is His first stroke in shaping you as a person.

- One translation uses words expressing David's awe at the complexity of his personal makeup, and without hesitation he credits the Master.

ACT3 Participant Guide

David, the Psalmist, declared that God had created his inmost being—that *God had knit him together in his mother's womb. David praised God because, as his Creator, He had made him wonderfully complex and that His workmanship was marvelous.* You are no exception. God wove your personality traits and natural talents into your DNA, long before you prayed to receive new life in Christ.

Those qualities, which your Heavenly Father infused into your unique temperament, have been detected and confirmed with your results from the personal strengths assessment. The **Strengths** point of your *Calling Star* comes into focus as you discover and understand your natural strengths and talents.

INTRODUCTION TO TALENTS & STRENGTHS

All people have a unique combination of talents, knowledge, and skills that they use in their daily lives to do their work, achieve their goals, and interact with others. While skills and knowledge can be acquired, you are born with your **Talents**. These naturally occurring behaviors, ways of thinking, personality nuances, and feelings are how you were fearfully and wonderfully made by God. When you spend time, energy, and other resources to grow your **Talents**, that is when those **Talents** become **Strengths**.

Can you think of someone who has a very clear God-given Talent who has invested in it to make it a Strength?

Even though we're all born with **Talents**, many people don't really know what their **Talents** are and therefore don't focus on using them every day. Instead, many people tend to focus on fixing their weaknesses or becoming someone that they are not created to be. By exploring your **Talents**, you can identify and build on the areas where you have infinite potential to grow and succeed as you look to fulfill your calling.

> Identifying your **Strengths** is not intended to take the place of identifying your **Spiritual Gifts**, but rather, it can be a powerful way to enhance your gifts and calling.

36

INTRODUCTION TO NATURAL TALENTS & PERSONALITY TRAITS

Teaching Points:

	35 Min	Start Time:
		End Time:

General Observations

- Our personality and natural talents drive how we interact with people and solve problems.

- The fascination with the human personality and natural talents is well documented for millennia. The multiple assessment tools that work to classify those traits all follow the study of the genius of our Master Creator.

- The Master did not simply care about making us unique as an expression of His limitless creativity; He brilliantly created a social system that demanded mutual respect, relationship, and interdependence.

- God designed us to want, enjoy, and need each other to maximize our human experience.

- Since we are intentionally designed to be interdependent, we must find ways to get along with all kinds of people in all kinds of situations.

- The Fall in the Garden created lots of problems, but among them is that we are naturally self-centered and want to be independent. God has specifically endowed and gifted some people with relational skills to connect and motivate others to counterbalance that general influence.

- God knew that we would have to solve the problems we encounter as we live out our lives in a broken world and work to find ways to make life better.

- He knew that the problems of a broken world would be complex and require more than any one person could bring to the table. So, He naturally endowed and spiritually gifted some people with the capacities to gather and process information with the intent to make decisions and design plans. To ensure that the plans are put into place, He also similarly capacitated some to energize themselves and others toward the execution of those plans and the desired results.

Discretionary Examples of God's Design Based on Uniqueness and Interdependence

- The first clue of God's intentional design of human uniqueness is in the account of Creation as recorded in Genesis.

  - Adam and Eve were created to be unique.

  - The first stated Ephesians 2:10 role for Eve was for relational purposes. Genesis 2:18: "It is not good for man to be alone."

  - *Helper*: Eve was made as a complimentary helper for Adam.

  - *Suitable*: The word means counterpart.

- The metaphor of the Body to describe the interdependencies of the Church.

  - Scriptures that deal with the complexity and symmetry of the Church use the description of the body as a favorite word picture.

  - The metaphor of the body speaks of our relational interdependence.

  - The metaphor describes the unique capacities of every part, the indispensable role that individual part plays, while at the same time pointing to the need of every other unique part that surrounds it.

  - The hand and the feet are identified as distinct in role but one in how they serve the purpose of the body.

  - The eyes and the ears are identified as distinct in their roles, but each as indispensable to the healthy functioning of the body.

o   Some of the roles are out front and seemingly more naturally honored; while those behind the scenes and less lauded are actually indispensable.

Summary Principles of Natural Talents and Personality Traits

- All of us are required to get along with people. But some are given natural talents to create warm, winsome, and relational environments, and relate to others in ways that form deeply meaningful and strong personal relationships.

- All of us are required to think and problem-solve. But some are equipped to get a group over-the-top with their God-given talent to look at problems, gather information, process the situation, and come up with a best way forward through strategic thinking.

- All of us are required to lead at least someone at some level in everyday life. But some are equipped by God to motivate and influence others to action for the common cause in a powerful way.

- All of us are required to appreciate history, honor the culture, live dependably in responsibilities, and follow through on plans. But some are gifted with an internal gyroscope to maintain stability and a heading in chaos. Some are a human machine that can't keep from turning plans into practice.

Assessments

- You demonstrate the genius of God as you live true to your natural talents and personality traits. When you develop and exercise the talents and traits the Master has laid in your foundation as a unique human being, you literally make every people group stronger. In the areas of your talents and traits, you add value to the group and increase their capacity to attract and embrace others, as well as strengthen a community's capacity to identify the issues and help to solve their shared problems.

- The purpose of assessments is to help give definition to a person's innate natural ways of thinking, feeling, and behaving.

- Use the handout provided by the local ACT3 Discovery Team outlining the basic tenets of the assessment used to identify the natural strengths and personality traits of the participant.

PERSONAL STRENGTHS ASSESSMENT - GROUP COACHING SEGMENT NOTES:

ACT3 Participant Guide

ADDITIONAL NOTES:

38

PERSONAL SHARING & BREAK

- Looking at the results of the strengths assessment you took, with which of your **Talents** do you most strongly identify? Why?

- Can you identify a time in your life when you saw this **Talent** as a **Strength** that God leveraged?

- Just because these are our talents, it doesn't mean that we are always comfortable with our natural inclinations.

    o *Which of your talents is your favorite? Why?*

    o *Which of your talents can drive you (and perhaps sometimes others around you) crazy? Why?*

    o *Which talent have you heard about that you may wish you had more of? Why?*

39

PERSONAL SHARING & BREAK

55 Min	Start Time:
	End Time:

Teaching Points:

- Encourage the participants to create pairs and share their Strengths Insights Report.

- Lead them at 20 minutes into a break; consider a 5-minute notice.

- Break can be shortened to realign with original schedule. Give permission to blend the personal sharing with the time allotted for the break at their discretion.

- At the end of the break, call them to re-gather for the 2nd round of facilitation. Consider a 5-minute notice.

ACT3 Participant Guide

DREAMING: OUT-OF-THE-BOX RETHINKING
Unlocking the heart

Acts 2:17
In the last days, God says, "I will pour out my Spirit on all people. Your sons and daughters will prophesy, your young men will see visions, your old men will dream dreams."

The context of this verse was the exciting time of Pentecost in Jerusalem after Jesus had ascended back to heaven. It is a powerful illustration of what can happen as our Ephesians 1:15-17 prayer gets answered! It was the day the *Spirit of wisdom and revelation* was "*poured out,*" the Church was birthed, and believers were transformed and sent forth to bless the world.

The foundational prayer of your ACT3 experience is Paul's prayer for the Ephesians. As the Spirit of wisdom and revelation helps you to know God better, your sensitivity to His plans for your life gets more detailed and your trust grows deeper for when He calls you beyond your comfort levels. Acts 2:17 sheds the light of expectation that God may have an "**out-of-the-box dream**" you've never dared to live before now. A dream doesn't have to be the latest, greatest ministry, but an insight that is new to you, in how to respond to a need that has caught your heart. It could also be a dream you've never dared to share before now, and your heart is being freshly stirred to act.

🧑‍🤝‍🧑 TABLE TALK

Have you ever had a sense that God has given you a dream—a task, or a sense of calling for a lifetime? What did it feel or look like? What gave you the sense that it included God's presence?

 PRAYING TOGETHER

Exchange nametags with someone at your table and pray for them

- Ask what ONE thing you could pray for them this week that would be helpful.

- Pray that the Holy Spirit would renew them and help them to know their calling.

- Pray that they would discover opportunities to serve consistent with their calling.

40

DREAMING: OUT-OF-THE-BOX RETHINKING

⏳ 10 Min	Start Time:
	End Time:

BIG IDEA

One of the signs of the indwelling of the Holy Spirit is *out-of-the-box thinking*. The same Spirit of Wisdom and Revelation in Ephesians 1 can whisper to our soul a sense of calling that goes beyond the conventional to meet a need.

DESIRED OUTCOME

- To encourage people to share an intuitive ministry that they have never shared, and to give God a chance to speak to their hearts about a ministry that doesn't yet exist.

Teaching Points:

- The fire-burst of Pentecost was the birth of the Church and the day the lights came on for a world in the dark.

- The connection to the Ephesians 1:15-17 prayer.

- The counterintuitive promise of Joel that Holy Spirit would make dreamers of 3rd Stagers, and the undeniable evidence that Pentecost initiated its fulfillment to this day.

TABLE TALK

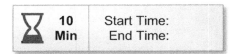

10 Min	Start Time: End Time:

PRAYING TOGETHER

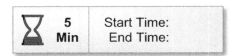

5 Min	Start Time: End Time:

Teaching Points:

- Urge them to find a prayer partner and exchange nametags.

- Encourage them to share one prayer request and pray for that need.

Additional Notes:

HOMEWORK

- Use the information you gathered from the person with whom you exchanged a nametag and pray for that person every day this week.

- Spend some time prayerfully reflecting on the personal strengths assessment you completed and complete the **Strengths Worksheet** (p. 43).

- Complete the **Spiritual Gifts Assessment** (p. 47).

- As you complete the **Strengths Worksheet**, go back to the map of your **Journey** (p. 25). Ask the Holy Spirit to identify the times that He has used your **Strengths** to make a difference in His Kingdom. Use the insights provided by Him to complete the **Strengths** point of your *Calling Star* (p. xiii).

CLOSING PRAYER

41

ACT3 Participant Guide

 GOING DEEPER

Balconies & Basements

Since talents come naturally to us, we must be aware that we can both under- and over-utilize **Talents** and even **Strengths**.

Go to YouTube and search "Gallup Theme Thursday Short - Balconies and Basements Explained" or go to the following link: www.bit.ly/balconiesandbasements

42

Strengths Worksheet

Reflect on the following questions and write down your responses. Next week we will spend some time sharing one-on-one, as well as sharing around your table, some of your responses to these challenging yet critical questions.

- What are some of your **Talents** that you recognize as **Strengths** that God has used in your life? What are ways in which you have invested in these **Talents** to grow them into **Strengths**?

- How have they been part of your **Journey** or played a role in the journey of others around you? Indicate these points on the map of your **Journey**.

- How might these **Talents** and **Strengths** play a role as you discover your calling and obey Him by serving?

*Pray and reflect on your **Talents** and **Strengths**. Ask God to show you which He intends to leverage as **Strengths** for your future as you serve in His Kingdom.*

*Write these 1-2 talents on the **Strengths** part of your Calling Star (p. xiii).*

43

Understanding Spiritual Gifts

Jesus was empowered by the Holy Spirit to do ministry as He lived out His purpose and served people while He while on the earth. Jesus made a mind-boggling statement that one day Christians would do even greater ministry than He did (John 14:2). Certainly, He never meant to infer that Christians are greater than Him. But He did lay the foundation for the future impact of the Church as each member would be individually gifted and empowered by the Holy Spirit, which would generate an exponential effect.

The Church is a team made up of people who are each uniquely equipped to minister like Jesus. Our personal ministry is therefore the continuation of Jesus' ministry. And the same Holy Spirit who empowered Him has endued you with some of the same abilities and power to serve today.

THE GIFTS

Spiritual gifts are discussed and listed in the following passages of the New Testament: 1 Corinthians 12:8-10; 12:28; Romans 12:6-8; Ephesians 4:11; and 1 Peter 4:11. **Since these lists are not duplicative, there are likely more gifts than the ones described in these passages**. *Additionally, for our purposes, ACT3 exists to connect people with opportunities to serve, which has resulted in our refined list that match most church teams and community service organizations.*

CATEGORIES OF SPIRITUAL GIFTS

The Apostle speaks of the variety of spiritual gifts: "Now there are different kinds of gifts, but the same Spirit. And there are different kinds of service, but the same Lord. There are different kinds of working, but the same God works all of them in all men.... All of these are the work of one and the same Spirit, and He gives them to each one, just as He determines" (1 Corinthians 12:4-11).

In a study of spiritual gifts, it is helpful to recognize different categories of spiritual gifts that are described in Scripture:

- **Motivational Gifts**: How God works in a believer to shape his or her perspective on life and motivate his or her words and actions.

- **Ministry Gifts**: How God works with what a believer does to serve and meet the needs of others.

- **Manifestation Gifts**: How God works through a believer in a given situation to demonstrate His supernatural power.

44

Motivational Gifts

The motivational gifts include gifts such as: faith, prophecy, serving, teaching, exhorting, giving, organizing, and mercy. These gifts of God's grace shape how the believer views life, relates to others, and impacts the Body of Christ. A motivational gift can be compared to a set of eyeglasses from God, given so that the believer can see people and circumstances through that particular set of "lenses."

Following are simple descriptions of motivational gifts, explaining how a person with each gift would "see" his or her role in the Body of Christ:

- Faith: Takes the lead and encourages others in acting on God's promises with confidence and unwavering belief in God's ability to fulfill His purposes

- Prophecy: Reveals truth by exposing sin, so that fellowship with God can be restored and/or maintained

- Serving/Helping: Demonstrates love by meeting practical needs, usually through tangible work

- Teaching: Discovers and validates truth so that the Church maintains accuracy

- Encouragement: Encourages Christians to grow spiritually by discipling, teaching, and counseling others

- Giving: Conserves and shares resources in order to meet needs

- Leadership: Carries out projects by recruiting workers, organizing tasks, or delegating responsibilities

- Mercy: Demonstrates God's love and compassion by responding to hurt

Ministry Gifts

Ministry gifts are the tools that God uses to build up the church. They are practical, essential, can-do types of gifts such as those described in Ephesians 4:11-13. Many times they are the people singled out for church leadership positions and ministry leaders.

Manifestation Gifts

Manifestation gifts are supernatural demonstrations of the Holy Spirit's presence and power. The Spirit of God is the Source of these gifts, and they are manifested for the benefit of others to bring God glory (1 Corinthians 12:4-11).

THE VALUE OF UNDERSTANDING SPIRITUAL GIFTS

Knowing that each Christian has gift sets that are unique, valuable, and needed in the Body of Christ gives believers purpose in God's kingdom.

ACT3 Participant Guide

1 Corinthians 12:17-25
If the whole body were an eye, where would the sense of hearing be? If the whole body were an ear, where would the sense of smell be? [18]But in fact God has arranged the parts in the body, every one of them just as He wants them to be. [19]If they were all one part, where would the body be? [20]As it is, there are many parts, but one body. [21]The eye cannot say to the hand, "I don't need you" And the head cannot say to the feet "I don't need you!" …[25]there should be no division in the body, but that its parts should have equal concern for each other.

SPIRITUAL GIFTS EXIST TO BENEFIT THE WHOLE CHURCH

1 Corinthians 12:7
"Now to each one the manifestation of the Spirit is given for the common good."

SPIRITUAL GIFTS ARE ALLOCATED BY GOD
The spiritual gifts are given by God's choice; we cannot choose our gifts. Because He is working within His master plan, His appointment of those gifts to an individual can also help to serve as a clue to the work He has called them to do. The converse is also true—a sense of calling can serve as a clue to the anticipation of the spiritual gifts He has given.

SPIRITUAL GIFTS ARE OFTEN MISUNDERSTOOD

- Spiritual gifts differ from natural talents and skills

- Not only are we given different gifts, but we are also given different measures of those gifts

- God will also give us passions and opportunities in addition to our strengths and spiritual gifts

- We must be willing to serve outside of our area of gifting when the circumstances warrant

- No list of spiritual gifts in the New Testament seems altogether complete and compiling all of the lists together still may not result in a complete list

46

Spiritual Gifts Assessment - Questions

1. I like organizing services and events

2. I can tell when someone is insincere

3. I pray for the lost daily

4. Encouraging others is a high priority in my life

5. Believing God for my daily needs is important to me

6. Influencing others for the kingdom of God through finances is extremely important to me

7. Having people over to my house is something I do often

8. Spending hours in prayer for other people is very enjoyable to me

9. People seek me out to learn more about the Kingdom of God

10. I tend to motivate others to get involved

11. My heart hurts when I see others hurting

12. Caring for the hurting is one of my highest priorities

13. I enjoy serving behind the scenes

14. I like creating outlines of the Bible

15. I am passionate about managing details

16. I sense when situations are spiritually unhealthy

17. I am greatly concerned about seeing the lost saved

18. I try to come across as loving and caring

19. Asking God for a list of big things is exciting to me

20. I find ways to give offerings above my tithe

21. Creating a warm and welcoming home is important to me

22. I am burdened to pray for situations in the world

23. Sometimes I sense the Holy Spirit helps me to "know" details in important circumstances I couldn't naturally know

24. I prefer to take the lead whenever necessary

25. I'm very sensitive to sad stories

26. I enjoy connecting, caring for and coaching others

27. It bothers me when people sit around and do nothing

28. I share Biblical truth with others in hopes of their personal growth

29. Creating a task list is easy and enjoyable for me

30. I can pinpoint issues or problems before others

31. I enjoy sharing the gospel with a total stranger

32. I look for ways to be an encouragement to other people

33. I trust that God has my back in every situation

47

80

ACT3 Participant Guide

34. Making more money means that I can give more

35. I tend to make total strangers feel at home

36. People often describe me as a prayer warrior

37. I work hard at knowing biblical details and helping others to understand and apply them in challenging circumstances

38. I delegate responsibilities to accomplish tasks

39. I am motivated to help those who are less fortunate

40. I enjoy walking with someone in times of difficulty

41. I like to do small things that others pass over

42. When I study scripture, God gives me unique insights

48

Spiritual Gifts Assessment - Score Sheet

RATING SCALE		
1 – Almost Never	3 – Sometimes	5 – Almost Always

			TOTAL	GIFT
1. ___	15. ___	29. ___	_____	A. _____
2. ___	16. ___	30. ___	_____	B. _____
3. ___	17. ___	31. ___	_____	C. _____
4. ___	18. ___	32. ___	_____	D. _____
5. ___	19. ___	33. ___	_____	E. _____
6. ___	20. ___	34. ___	_____	F. _____
7. ___	21. ___	35. ___	_____	G. _____
8. ___	22. ___	36. ___	_____	H. _____
9. ___	23. ___	37. ___	_____	I. _____
10. ___	24. ___	38. ___	_____	J. _____
11. ___	25. ___	39. ___	_____	K. _____
12. ___	26. ___	40. ___	_____	L. _____
13. ___	27. ___	41. ___	_____	M. _____
14. ___	28. ___	42. ___	_____	N. _____

49

82

Spiritual Gifts Assessment - Key

A. Administration

B. Discernment

C. Evangelism

D. Encouragement

E. Faith

F. Giving

G. Hospitality

H. Intercession

I. Knowledge

J. Leadership

K. Mercy

L. Shepherding

M. Serving/Helping

N. Teaching

Spiritual Gifts Application Guide

THE SPIRITUAL GIFT OF ADMINISTRATION

The Gift of Administration is the divine strength or ability to give direction and make decisions on behalf of others that result in efficient operation and accomplishment of goals. Administration includes the ability to organize people, things, information, finances, etc.

People with the Gift of Administration are strong on detail. They know how to take the pertinent details of a situation, and in light of the mission, put a plan on paper and start delegating responsibility.

(Luke 14:28-30; Acts 6:1-7; 1 Corinthians 12:28)

Do You Have This Gift?
- Do things like efficiency and promptness matter more to you than to most people?

- Do you get agitated when things seem poorly organized and you want to fix them?

- Can you bring order out of chaos?

- Do you naturally organize your life, schedule, finances, priorities, etc.?

- Do you naturally focus on the best possible utilization of available resources?

- Do you like to make decisions about *what should be done* and *when it should be done*?

- Do you enjoy formulating plans, framing policies and setting objectives?

Potential Ways To Use This Gift
- Chairperson or Member of a planning team

- Teams coordinator

- Volunteer coordinator

- Event organizer

- Administrative assistant

- Data management

51

ACT3 Participant Guide

THE SPIRITUAL GIFT OF DISCERNMENT

The Gift of Discernment is the God-given ability to quickly and clearly recognize and distinguish between the influence of God, Satan, the world, and the flesh in a given situation. People with the Gift of Discernment recognize what is genuine from what is pretense, what is counterfeit from what is real.

(Matthew 16:21-23; Acts 5:1-11, 16:16-18; 1 Corinthians 12:10; 1 John 4:1-6)

Do You Have This Gift?
- Do you feel a special responsibility to protect the truth of God's Word by exposing error?

- Do you often make a swift evaluation of someone or something that was said, that others did not see but yet proved to be correct?

- Do you perceive deception in others and it later proves to be correct?

- Do you recognize inconsistencies between words and actions?

- Are you mindful of moral sin and doctrinal heresy?

- Can you quickly detect any false teaching while listening to a speaker or reading a book?

- Are you sensitive to demonic presence and able to help people be free from demons?

Potential Ways To Use This Gift
- Member of a decision-making team

- Church officer or board of Elders member

- Member of a Counseling ministry

- Consultant to those who make ministry decisions

THE SPIRITUAL GIFT OF EVANGELISM

The Gift of Evangelism is the divine strength or ability to help non-Christians take the necessary steps to become Christ followers.

People with the Gift of Evangelism care passionately about lost people and want to help them know Jesus. They are driven to understand the questions and doubts of lost people so that they can provide compelling answers. A person with this gift often prefers being with people in the culture, or even outside of the culture, rather than

52

hanging out with Christians in the church.

(Acts 8:5-6, 8:26-40, 14:21, 21:8; Ephesians 4:11-14)

Do You Have This Gift?

- Do you find it natural to direct a conversation toward the topic of Jesus Christ?

- Do you enjoy being with non-Christians and sharing the gospel?

- Do you effectively communicate to non-Christians in a language they can understand?

- Does it bring you deep joy when a person crosses the line of faith?

- Do you like to equip others to share their faith?

- Do you find yourself being burdened for the spiritual condition of those of another culture?

Potential Ways To Use This Gift

- Local outreach events

- Mission trips

- Local ministries to immigrants or other resident nationalities

- Personal faith-sharing in conversational settings

THE SPIRITUAL GIFT OF ENCOURAGEMENT

The Gift of Encouragement is the divine strength or ability to encourage others by conversation, with written notes, and through acts of service and kindness. Encouragers are people oriented, discipleship oriented, and growth oriented. The person with this gift can usually recognize the potential of another person and can envision that his or her spiritual achievement. Encouragers are process oriented and understand the steps necessary for people to apply truth and make progress in their spiritual maturity.

People with the Gift of Encouragement have an unusual sensitivity to those who are discouraged or struggling. These people also tend to have a high capacity of patience and optimism.

(Acts 14:22; Romans 12:8; 1 Timothy 4:13; Hebrews 10:24-25)

53

ACT3 Participant Guide

Do You Have This Gift?

- Do you love to see others mature in their faith?

- Do you desire for others to discover their Spiritual DNA and leverage their resources to live in alignment with their calling?

- Are you conscious of your example because you want to be a model for others?

- Do people who are struggling seek you out for advice and encouragement?

- Are you naturally mindful of those who are suffering and struggling?

- Do you enjoy walking with someone through difficulties, because you believe they can grow through suffering?

- Are you especially patient with people?

Potential Ways To Use This Gift

- Join the discipling teams of your church

- Offer yourself to make early contact with brand new believers

- Join a team that helps people discover their Spiritual DNA and find opportunities to use their capacities

- Ask for believers who are struggling with long term challenges

- Make yourself available to visit or make phone calls to the sick or elderly who are home-bound or in residential care

- Join the prayer ministry

- Ask pastoral care for a card-writing role for those struggling, suffering loss, or celebrating milestones

- Join volunteer appreciation events or teams

THE SPIRITUAL GIFT OF FAITH

The Gift of Faith is the ability to envision what needs to be done and to trust God to accomplish the seemingly impossible. The person with the gift of faith is enabled to act on God's promises with extraordinary confidence and an unwavering belief in God's ability to fulfill His promises.

People with the Gift of Faith trust God in tough circumstances when others are ready to give up. These people are often visionaries who dream big dreams, pray big

54

prayers, and attempt big things for Jesus. These people tend to be optimistic, change-oriented, and future-focused. They believe the promises of God and inspire others to do the same.

(Acts 11:22-24; Romans 4:18-21; 1 Corinthians 12:9; Hebrews 11)

Do You Have This Gift?

- Do you view obstacles as opportunities and trust God for the impossible?

- Do you enjoy pointing others to examples of the power of God intervening in seemingly impossible circumstances?

- Do people who doubt the possibility of God performing the miraculous tick you off?

- When people have their backs against the wall, do they specifically want you praying for them?

- Do you maintain lists of prayer needs and the answers to prayers?

Potential Ways To Use This Gift

- Join organized prayer teams for public praying

- Join organized prayer teams for leadership team support

- Join organized prayer teams for specific needs of children, students, or adults

- Offer to be personal prayer partner for specific leaders

- Join the discipleship team to teach the power of faith to new believers

- Offer written or public testimonies of Divine intervention to the communications team

- Tell your stories of God's power on social media

- Join the leadership teams of new start ministries

- Support mission outreaches

THE SPIRITUAL GIFT OF GIVING

The Gift of Giving is the ability to give money and other forms of wealth joyfully, wisely, and generously to meet the needs of others and help support ministries. People with this gift do not ask, "How much money do I need to give to God?" but rather "How much money do I need to live on?" with the intent of giving much of the rest away. The person with the gift of giving rejoices when he or she perceives that his or her giving is an answer to someone else's prayer.

People with the Gift of Giving genuinely view themselves as stewards and that everything belongs to God. It is not uncommon for this gift to be accompanied by the ability to produce wealth, though certainly not a requirement.

(Mark 12:41-44; Romans 12:8; 2 Corinthians 8:1-7, 9:2-7)

Do You Have This Gift?
- Do you tend to see the needs of others more than other people do?

- Do you see giving to a worthwhile project as an exciting honor and privilege?

- Do you give with a sense of investment and an anticipation of Kingdom ROI?

- Are you eager to motivate others to give?

- Do you intently look for ways to see a need met?

Potential Ways To Use This Gift
- Connect with under-resourced ministries to the poor and powerless

- Provide support for mission projects and missionaries

- Lead or help with fundraising projects

- Share testimonies of how God has provided for your needs

- Establish trust accounts and foundations to provide ongoing resources for ministry

THE SPIRITUAL GIFT OF HOSPITALITY

The Gift of Hospitality is the divine strength or ability to create warm, welcoming environments to welcome strangers and entertain guests in a home, an office, the church, or other gathering places. People with the Gift of Hospitality tend to have an "open home" where others are welcome to visit.

(Acts 16:14-15; Romans 12:13, 16:23; Hebrews 13:1-2; 1 Peter 4:9)

Do You Have This Gift?
- Do you enjoy having people in your home?

- Do you enjoy watching people interact in warm and inviting gatherings you help to plan and host?

56

- Did you choose or design your home with entertaining visitors in mind?

- Do most people feel comfortable to drop by and visit unannounced?

Potential Ways To Use This Gift
- Host a small group Bible study

- Offer your home as a meeting place for student ministries, or kids groups to meet

- Offer your home to leadership to be used for meetings or new attendees

THE SPIRITUAL GIFT OF INTERCESSION

The Gift of Intercession is the divine strength or ability to stand in the gap in prayer for someone, something, or someplace, believing for profound results. This gift is the special enablement that God gives to certain members of the Body of Christ to pray (especially on behalf of and for others) for extended periods of time on a regular basis and see frequent and specific answers to their prayers.

(Hebrews 7:25; Colossians 1:9-12; 4:12-13; James 5:14-16)

Do You Have This Gift?
- Do you see some of the issues in people's lives as challenges that can only be fully resolved through prayer?

- Do you set a daily time to pray for spiritual victories over the challenges and obstacles of others?

- Do you pray in response to a leading from God, whether understood or not?

- Do you believe that the work of Satan and the demonic can be resisted in the lives of people, ministries, and world circumstances through prayer?

- Do you find yourself unwilling to settle for the challenging circumstances in people's lives that look to be beyond the help of natural resolution?

Potential Ways To Use This Gift
- Join organized prayer teams for public praying

- Join organized prayer teams for leadership team support

- Join organized prayer teams for specific needs of children, students, or adults

- Offer to be a personal prayer partner for specific leaders

57

ACT3 Participant Guide

- Offer to be a prayer warrior with access to list of the needs of your church and its people

- Participate at some level in the National Day of Prayer

THE SPIRITUAL GIFT OF KNOWLEDGE

The Gift of Knowledge is the God-given ability to learn, understand, remember, and recount insights from the Bible, the experiences of their life, and personal revelations by the Holy Spirit. People with the Gift of Knowledge not only archive in their minds the truths they have learned, but are also particularly sensitive to the voice of the Holy Spirit to reveal facts that are not knowable by normal study about individual circumstances. They are supernaturally aware of how God's Word connects to every situation and how it informs every decision a Christian makes.

(Acts 5:1-22; 1 Corinthians 12:8; Colossians 2:2-3)

Do You Have This Gift?
- Do you love to study and research the Bible for insight, understanding, and truth?

- Do you have a good memory that retains insights from God's Word and life experiences?

- Do you sometimes get an intuitive sense that leads to "knowing" a detail or insight that is only explainable by a word from the Holy Spirit?

- Do people often come to you with difficult problems and questions, seeking your insight because they know the Holy Spirit can use you to give insights to them?

Potential Ways To Use This Gift
- Become a member of a decision-making team

- Offer your help in counseling or teaching

- Provide research for those who present biblical messages

THE SPIRITUAL GIFT OF LEADERSHIP

The Gift of Leadership is the God-given ability to recognize a clear and significant vision from God, and then cast that vision and influence to other people to harmoniously accomplish that vision for the purposes of God.

People with the Gift of Leadership tend to gravitate toward the "point position" in a ministry. Others tend to have trust and confidence in their abilities. They best serve others by leading them. They tend to operate with a strong sense of destiny.

(Romans 12:8; 1 Timothy 3:1-13, 5:17; Hebrews 13:17)

Do You Have This Gift?

- Do others tend to naturally want to know what you think and go where you go?

- Do you enjoy being the "final voice" or the one with the overall responsibility for the direction and success of a group or organization?

- When a difficult situation arises, do others look to you for input and leadership?

- Do you usually take leadership in a group where none exists?

- Do you find leadership enjoyable rather than frustrating and difficult?

- Do others look to you to make major decisions for a group or organization?

Potential Ways To Use This Gift

- Become a leader within your church teams ministry or a community service organization

- Become a leader of a small group

- Offer your gift to your church leadership team

THE SPIRITUAL GIFT OF MERCY

The Gift of Mercy is the capacity to feel and express unusual compassion and sympathy for those in difficult or crisis situations and provide them with the necessary help and support to see them through tough times.

People with the Gift of Mercy are typically good listeners. They easily experience the pain of others. They want to make a difference in the lives of hurting people without being judgmental.

(Matthew 9:35-36; Mark 9:41; Romans 12:8; 1 Thessalonians 5:14)

Do You Have This Gift?

- Do you find yourself being drawn to people who are needy, hurting, sick, disabled, or elderly?

59

ACT3 Participant Guide

- Do you often think of ways to help those who are suffering?

- Is it unavoidable for you to experience compassion towards people having personal and emotional problems?

- Does helping the hurting energize you or depress you?

- Do you find yourself responding to people more out of compassion than judgment?

Potential Ways To Use This Gift

- Join a team that visits hospital patients and shut-ins

- Join a team that comes alongside of the homeless

- Offer your services to a food bank assistance program

- Get involved in recovery programs, prison ministry, or social justice causes

THE SPIRITUAL GIFT OF SHEPHERDING

The Gift of Pastoring/Shepherding is the divine strength or ability to assume long-term personal responsibility for the spiritual welfare of an individual or group of believers by nurturing and guiding them toward ongoing spiritual maturity. The person with a shepherd's heart has a love for people that compels them to meet with people to care for them and guide them with biblical instruction. People with this gift find great joy in seeing people mature in their faith and overcome besetting sin and discouragement.

(John 10:1-18; Ephesians 4:11-14; 1 Timothy 3:1-7; 1 Peter 5:1-3)

Do You Have This Gift?

- Do you have a deep love for people that compels you to care for them?

- Do you enjoy meeting with people to listen to their life story and provide them biblical insights?

- When you hear that someone is hurting, is your first instinct to try to be of help?

- Are you able to point out sin in someone's life in a loving way that they receive as helpful?

- Do you enjoy discipling newer believers?

60

Potential Ways To Use This Gift

- Become a small group leader

- Join the children's ministry or student ministry

- Join community service ministries that come alongside of those in need.

- Look for groups where people are gathering with specific needs

THE SPIRITUAL GIFT OF SERVING/HELPING

The Gift of Serving/Helping is the God-given ability to joyfully work alongside another and help that person complete the task God has given them. A person with this gift serves most satisfactorily by doing tangible work. They are the precious, irreplaceable utility members of a strong team. People with this gift prefer to work behind the scenes. They also tend to find joy in helping alleviate the burdens and responsibilities of others. This gift is usually accompanied with an attitude of humility and sacrifice, as well as an ability to perceive the needs of others. Availability is one of the server's strongest character qualities. A person with this gift almost never says no when asked to help others.

People with the Gift of Serving/Helping tend to demonstrate a servant attitude, loyalty, attention to detail, and responsiveness to the initiatives of others. They function well in positions of detail and assistant leadership.

(Acts 6:1-6, 9:36; Romans 12:7, 16:1-2; 1 Corinthians 12:28; 1 Timothy 1:16-18; Titus 3:14)

Do You Have This Gift?

- Do you enjoy helping others become more effective in their work?

- Do you enjoy, maybe even prefer, short-term tasks?

- Do you prefer to work behind the scenes?

- When someone is doing a job poorly, is your first instinct to help them instead of criticize?

- Do you prefer to work in a supportive rather than a leadership capacity?

- When you hear of someone with needs, do you offer your services if possible?

Potential Ways To Use This Gift

- Make yourself available to SOS (emergency fill-ins) needs for weekend services

- Join the events team for setup and teardown

61

ACT3 Participant Guide

- Look for church and community service projects

- Join the guest service team

- Become an office assistant

- Join the grounds or maintenance team

THE SPIRITUAL GIFT OF TEACHING

The Gift of Teaching is the divine ability and desire to study and learn from God's Word and make the Truth clear with accuracy and simplicity.

People with the Gift of Teaching enjoy learning, researching, communicating, and illustrating the truth of Scripture. These people enjoy studying and learning new information, and find great joy in sharing it with others. The spiritually gifted teacher has great adaptability as to the format, which can vary from one-on-one discipleship to formal classes, informal Bible studies, large groups, and preaching. The spiritually gifted teacher will usually become a teacher of teachers.

(Acts 18:24-28, 20:20-21; 1 Corinthians 12:28; Ephesians 4:11-14)

Do You Have This Gift?
- Do you enjoy studying and researching?

- Do you enjoy sharing biblical truth with others?

- Do others come to you for insight into Scripture?

- When you teach, do people "get it?"

- When you see someone confused in their understanding of the Bible do you feel a responsibility to speak to them about it?

- Do you enjoy speaking to various sized groups about biblical issues for which you have strong convictions?

Potential Ways To Use This Gift
- Become a Bible teacher to children, students, or adults

- Become a teaching coach, teaching other teachers

- Make yourself available for input to the congregational teaching team

- Join a teaching team at the congregational level

62

- Become a teacher's assistant

- Become a tutor to children, students, or adults (cultural or cross-cultural)

ACT3 Participant Guide

ADDITIONAL NOTES ON SPIRITUAL GIFTS:

64

Week 4 at a Glance
ReCommitting to Spiritual Gifts and Relationships

OUTCOMES

- Develop an understanding of Spiritual Gifts and their supercharged nature.
- Solidify the value of the participant's Spiritual Gifts through peer sharing.
- Establish the value of relationships in accomplishing the Master's work.
- Reinstate a sense of personal worth for those suffering experiences that have dinged and scarred them.
- Continue to raise the value of finished homework and a completed *Calling Star*.

AGENDA

WELCOME AND OPENING PRAYER		
The Master's Stroke of Spiritual Gifts	• 1 Corinthians 12:4-11 • The powerful additions at salvation • 1 Peter 4:10 • The purpose of Spiritual Gifts	**Time:** 25 minutes
Personal Sharing of Spiritual Gifts	• What are your Spiritual Gifts? • When has God used you in those gifts?	**Time:** 15 minutes
The Master's use of People in our Development	• 1 Timothy 4:12, 14; 2 Timothy 1:5-7 • God's use of family, friends, and disciplers • The power of the words they speak	**Time:** 15 minutes
Table Talk	• People God has used in your life • Words they spoke that shaped you • Who can God use to speak to you now?	**Time:** 10 minutes
BREAK		**Time: 15 minutes**
ReThinking Your Worth	• Psalms 19:1; 2 Chronicles 7:1 • The meaning of *kabod*	**Time:** 5 minutes
The Impact of Kabod	• Illustration of the nicked-up nickel	**Time:** 10 minutes
Restoring Lost Kabod	• Isaiah 6:1-8 • The power of worship	**Time:** 5 minutes
Table Talk	• How and why do you feel nicked-up? • In what areas are you feeling worth-less?	**Time:** 10 minutes
Homework	• Record top 3 **Spiritual Gifts** in *Calling Star* • Complete People Worksheet	**Time:** 5 minutes

	• Complete Passions Worksheet	

Reminders:

- Start as close to the designated time as possible.

- As you welcome, remind the group of our purpose: *To connect 3rd Stagers to people and opportunities to serve in alignment with their calling.*

- Reinforce the pivotal role of homework in the Discovery process and the next steps in connecting to opportunities to serve.

- Encourage them to stay current with their *Calling Star.*

Week 4: ReCommitting to Spiritual Gifts and Relationships

OPENING PRAYER

SPIRITUAL GIFTS
'Others-focused' talents given by the Holy Spirit upon accepting Christ

1 Corinthians 12:4-11
There are different kinds of gifts, but the same Spirit. ⁵There are different kinds of service, but the same Lord. ⁶There are different kinds of working, but the same God works all of them in all men. ⁷Now to each one the manifestation of the Spirit is given for the common good. ⁸To one there is given through the Spirit the message of wisdom, to another the message of knowledge by means of the same Spirit, ⁹to another faith by the same Spirit, to another gifts of healing by that one Spirit, ¹⁰to another miraculous powers, to another prophecy, to another distinguishing between spirits, to another speaking in different kinds of tongues, and to still another the interpretation of tongues. ¹¹All these are the work of one and the same Spirit, and He gives them to each one, just as He determines.

We are introduced to God in the first verse of the Bible as the Creator of heaven and earth. That was not a one-and-done proposition for our Creator God. John records in John 5:17 that Jesus taught, *My Father is always at His work to this very day, and I, too, am working.*

Creator God caused the beauty of the universe and the awesome balance of nature.

65

SPIRITUAL GIFTS

20 Min	Start Time:
	End Time:

BIG IDEA

Spiritual Gifts are given by the Holy Spirit to serve the Church and advance the mission it has been assigned. The gifts reside in the individual, but belong to the Church for her benefit.

Recognition of the spiritual gifts the Holy Spirit has endowed, and of the guidance He promises will inevitably lead to both nurture and outreach. We are not waiting for the Holy Spirit for spiritual gifts. He is waiting for us to use them!

- To help people discover and understand the role of their own spiritual gifts in equipping them to meet needs in a supernatural partnership with God.

- To help people understand that the concept and use of spiritual gifts in serving is the genius of God to create interdependence, catalyze relationships, enhance effectiveness, and ensure unity in the Body.

Teaching Points:

- Read 1 Corinthians 12:4-11.

- Circle the word "gifts" in verse 4. *Charisma:* an endowment.

- Circle the word "manifestation" in verse 7. *Phanerosis:* to shine.

- Remind them that in creating the unique you, the foundational strokes of the Master's brush took place before your first breath while in your mother's womb.

- Point out that His brush has never left the canvas as He uses the experiences of your life to add character, beauty, and depth to who you are.

- Celebrate the masterstroke that occurs at the rebirth of a new believer, triggered by the indwelling of the Holy Spirit. Something supernatural happened in that connecting moment with the Giver of Life.

- Point out that these are not just housewarming gifts from a God who is happy with you, or is rewarding you for your faith. They are the result of the spiritual DNA passed on to you through your born-again experience. These spiritual gifts make you most like your Heavenly Father.

- Emphasize that the Master is not done, but spiritual gifts will now serve to bring powerful experiences to your life that will take the beauty of your canvas to the masterpiece level!

ACT3 Participant Guide

David wrote in Psalms 19:1, *The heavens declare the glory of God; the skies proclaim the work of His hands.* Careful study would confirm that His work in the heavens and on earth is ongoing. That work is so structured and systematic that our study of His work is the foundation of all science.

Creator God is at work building the Church through Jesus Christ. Jesus told His disciples, *on this rock I will build my Church...* The Church is the collection of God's people on earth and the means through which He carries out His plans in the world. Though Pentecost was the birth of His Church, He continues to build it to this day. The ongoing work of Jesus includes building believers and fitting them into this beautiful and powerful body of people.

And Creator God is at work shaping and fitting you into the Church. His work in you is about connecting you relationally with other believers and functionally in how you contribute in the work of the whole.

God's work on who we are and how we relate to others is His ongoing dedication to our maturity. His work to fit us into His purposes was planned before our first breath, and it was energized when we accepted Christ and were filled with His Spirit.

Finding your fit is based on your understanding of how God has equipped you to best serve. So, finding your fit should therefore include a study of the **Spiritual Gifts**.

Michelangelo took years to sculpt David and paint the Sistine Chapel. God takes our lifetime to finish His work on us. But there are two major movements in God's work on you:

- The day you were given life and He fashioned your DNA from your parents. That day He determined the natural talents and abilities with which you would live your life.

- The day you were given eternal life through Faith and the gift of the Spirit. That day you were infused with the traits of your Heavenly Father through spiritual gifts.

In 1 Corinthians 12:4-11, Paul is describing what happens in the 2nd big movement of the Master in your life. As your DNA and personality traits form the basis for your resemblance to your earthly parents, your spiritual gifts form part of the basis of your resemblance to your Heavenly Father.

1 Peter 4:10
Each one should use whatever gift he has received to serve others, faithfully administering God's grace in its various forms.

Finding your place in serving as a 3rd Stager must include reassurance of how He has wired you for service. Once you know your gifts, Peter is clear—you should use

66

1 PETER 4:10

20 Min	Start Time:
	End Time:

Teaching Points:

- The concept of Spiritual Gifts does not exempt us from roles and responsibilities requiring all of the normal attributes of a believer. It clarifies that we are particularly gifted in some of those attributes.

  o For example, every believer navigates life through faith, while some have the Gift of Faith to amp up the flow of faith when circumstances in the Body demand it.

  o Another example is that every believer is required to be like their Heavenly Father in giving, while some exercise their Gift of Giving when circumstances in the Body and a broken world demand it.

  o The same concept is played out in teaching, mercy, helping, leadership, etc.

  o In some measure, every trait the Church will ever need lies inherently within us all individually, while the shortfall in any given circumstance being made up by special gifts lying resident in chosen individuals. And **every** person is chosen to steward one or more of those supernatural capacities.

- The chapters that contain lists of Spiritual Gifts are 1 Corinthians 12, 13, 14; Romans 12; Ephesians 4; 1 Peter 4.

- There is a reason God did not give any one person all of the spiritual gifts. We need to depend on each other. We need interdependence. Randy Frazee wrote: "Our limitations in the gifts create a need for interdependence, for our brothers and sisters to share with the community their gifts, as well as to keep us humble, because we cannot reach the world alone."

Facilitator Notes or Personal Story:

them! The purpose of the gifts is to serve others. When you serve, it is God working in real time in you. Letting God harness your natural strengths and employ your spiritual gifts to serve is the partnership God longs to experience with you.

> *"You are the only person on Earth who can use your ability."*
>
> Zig Ziglar

Holy Spirit + Spirit-filled Church + your spiritual gift = meeting needs and completing mission

Serving with your spiritual gifts creates the profound opportunity for you to experience the unique partnership with the Holy Spirit ministering to a specific need. You become part of an equation that is unbalanced without your involvement. You can't take you out of the equation without impacting the outcome.

 TABLE TALK: SHARING YOUR SPIRITUAL GIFTS

- What are your **Spiritual Gifts**? Is this a new discovery or reaffirmation for you?

- What is one area where God has called you (either in the past or now) to use one of your **Spiritual Gifts**?

 PEOPLE
Those who have spoken into your life and those who are speaking into your life now

 1 Timothy 4:12, 14
Don't let anyone look down on you because you are young, but set an example for the believers in speech, in life, in love, in faith, and in purity. [14]Do not neglect your gift, which was given you through a prophetic message when the body of elders laid their hands on you.

2 Timothy 1:5-7
I have been reminded of your sincere faith, which first lived in your grandmother Lois and in your mother Eunice and, I am persuaded, now

67

TABLE TALK: SHARING YOUR SPIRITUAL GIFTS

⧖	**15 Min**	Start Time: End Time:

- Ask participants to pair up to share their Spiritual Gifts assessment.

PEOPLE

⧖	**15 Min**	Start Time: End Time:

BIG IDEA

God has always used people as junior partners in His development and guidance for His people. Different individuals play different roles. They use a combination of their spiritual gifts as well as the position or relationship they have been given or you have entrusted to them.

DESIRED OUTCOME

- To encourage participants to stay aware of God's use of instrumental people in their lives and keep their hearts open to them. Along with their encouragement and direct acts of kindness and assistance, God sometimes uses people to speak a direct word that becomes pivotal for how we live our lives.

Teaching Points:

- Read 1 Timothy 4:12, 14. After reading, ask the group to circle the phrase "prophetic message" in the verse.

- Read 2 Timothy 1:5-7.

- Talk about the types of people God uses in our lives.

  - **God-friends**: People who prayed for him with the awareness that God had plans for him.

  - **Accountability partners**: People who know your calling, personality – both, strengths and vulnerabilities – and the God-moments you've experienced.

  - **Mentor**: People who work side-by-side or individually in different roles, yet for the same outcome: maturity and effectiveness in your calling.

- Teach them that God always uses partners in His work in our lives. He is very intentional about putting key people in your life. Identifying them serves to underscore the detailed involvement of God in your life.

- Emphasize the need to identify any particular words these friends have spoken that turned out to be life-shaping or life-directing words.

- Encourage them to plot on their Journey Map the entry points of these God-friends in their lives. Note any special stories that led to the relationship. Also advise them to add any of those "God-words" that these friends spoke to them. Like Paul reminded Timothy, sometimes those can be prophetic words when thinking about our calling and how to fulfill it.

- Caution them to the vulnerability of 3rd Stagers who lose contact with those God has used in the past, and urge them to expect God to add new friends they can trust that God can use to speak into their life today.

ACT3 Participant Guide

lives in you also. 6For this reason I remind you to fan into flame the gift of God, which is in you through the laying on of my hands. 7For God did not give us a spirit of timidity, but a spirit of power, of love and of self-discipline.

Identifying the God-Given Entourage for your Journey

We were never intended to travel alone in our walk to follow Christ. We really are better together. You can be sure that God has an entourage for you. Look at the people and their roles in Timothy's life. As we look at his God-given traveling companions, let God remind you of the people who have played similar roles in your life. If that list is thin, keep your eyes open and expect God to fill those roles in your life during this new season of opportunities.

In just these two passages in the letters Paul sent to Timothy, he identifies precious people in Timothy's life. The role of people is huge in God's development of our spiritual maturity.

Paul pens the classic passage of the powerful role of **family** in the formation of our Faith. Timothy's grandmother and mother were his **role models of faith**. People who play that role not only model, but they are also intentional about instilling the principles of faith in our thinking. Those relationships should be cherished and celebrated as you live out your calling. Those relationships should serve as models in your roles to the next generations of your family.

Paul states that Timothy had **God-friends**—people who prayed for him with the awareness that God had plans for him. They believed in him. They prayed strategically and fervently for him.

Paul, himself, plays the role of an **accountability partner** to Timothy. Paul knows Timothy's calling, his personality—both, strengths and vulnerabilities—and the God-moments he had experienced. Paul reminded Timothy of the milestones he had experienced, and Paul exhorted him to follow through with the calling God had assigned to him.

Paul also played the role of a **mentor**. With the intimate knowledge he had of Timothy, he invited him into opportunities to live out his calling with the gifts and strengths that God had given to him. They worked side-by-side, and they worked individually in different roles, yet for the same outcome—his maturity and effectiveness in his calling.

Remembering the God-Inspired Messages People Have Spoken

Paul is not talking about singing Kumbaya around the campfire in this passage. Paul wanted to take Timothy back to a tender moment when he *knew* he had heard from God. Paul didn't need to repeat everything that was said. All he needed to do was remind Timothy of the tender experience.

Paul chooses a Greek word in 4:14 that is here translated as a *prophetic message*. The

68

Week 4: ReCommitting to Spiritual Gifts and Relationships

word Paul uses signifies "the speaking forth of the mind and counsel of God." Timothy had heard from God through the voice of a trusted friend.

Remembering *what* was said to you in those precious "aha" experiences of life is as important as remembering *who* said them. The weight of *what* has been said is increased with the *depth* of your relationship with the person God used to speak them. We must always nurture the relationships God can use to speak a clarifying word to us in our lives.

 TABLE TALK

- Who are the people that have played a role in your life that are comparable to those that Paul identifies in Timothy's life? Who has God used in the past to speak into your life?

- What impacts did they have and what were the messages they spoke to you?

- Who is speaking into your life *now* to guide and encourage you as you discover your calling?

 BREAK

RETHINKING YOUR WORTH

Last week we talked about how we can begin to feel like a misfit in the very world we live in—out of place, out of step, or even off the radar with the people around us, almost like aliens in a foreign place. There is also a vulnerability to an even larger problem: What if, wherever we are in the world, we've begun to discount ourselves?

> *Psalms 19:1*
> *The heavens declare the **glory** of God; the skies proclaim the work of His hands.*

69

TABLE TALK

| ⏳ 10 Min | Start Time: |
| | End Time: |

BREAK

| ⏳ 15 Min | Start Time: |
| | End Time: |

RETHINKING YOUR WORTH

| ⏳ 5 Min | Start Time: |
| | End Time: |

BIG IDEA

The wear and tear of life will wear us down and scar us up, making us feel like we're worth "less" than we once did or a "lightweight" in the face of resistance. God has made provisions to renew and restore us back to our intended "weighty" usefulness.

DESIRED OUTCOME

- To encourage those in the group who feel like they have been used up, abused, discarded, or careless in life in a way that diminishes their worth and fear that they have blown any chance to be used by God.

- To encourage participants who have suffered from bad decisions or broken relationships and wonder if they can ever connect to people or be trusted with meaningful responsibilities again.

- To encourage those who feel used up and worn, or like a lightweight in a heavyweight fight, that there is hope for renewal.

Teaching Points:

- Before the segment begins, build anticipation by promising that this could be the most emotional point for some. It can also be a pivot point and breakthrough for some.

- Read Psalms 19:1 and 2 Chronicles 7:1.

- Ask the participants to circle the word "glory" in the verses above.

Facilitator Notes:

ACT3 Participant Guide

2 Chronicles 7:1

*When Solomon finished praying, fire came down from heaven and consumed the burnt offering and the sacrifices, and the **glory** of the Lord filled the temple.*

The word "glory" is used when translating the Hebrew word *"kabod"* in the Bible. Curiously, *kabod* is derived from a root with the basic meaning of "heavy." From this root came, among other things, a word meaning "rich." Speakers of ancient Hebrew would refer to a rich person as "heavy in wealth," much as we might say someone is loaded. A similar extension of the literal sense of *kabod* included being loaded with power, reputation, or honor. It's from this use of the word that we get the meaning of glory. God's glory is God's weightiness in wonderful qualities such as might, beauty, goodness, justice, honor, and power.

- The Psalmist, David, points to the abundant evidence of the invisible God's "weightiness" displayed in Creation.

- 2 Chronicles uses the word *kabod* to refer to the awesome presence of God at the Temple dedication.

- In 1 Samuel 4, we see in it in the Story of Ichabod, where the heartbreaking outcry is that the glory (*kabod*) has departed ("i" is a prefix for negation).

- The same word *kabod* is used to describe the weightiness, or worth, of Joseph as he had risen through the ranks of Egyptian leadership. He told his brothers to tell his father of his "glory," or *kabod*.

HOW IS YOUR *KABOD* THESE DAYS?
Are you feeling worth-less-ness or worth-i-ness?

The Bible records the story of Moses spending time alone with God during the writing of the Ten Commandments. Included in that epic story is the detail that God's glory, or *kabod*, rubbed off on Moses to the point that his body had a holy glow and his face was radiant when he came back down the mountain to rejoin the people.

But Paul uses the story in a stunning, yet practical way. He says that as time passed after Moses' encounter with the glory of God, the holy glow began a process of fading. Moses is so embarrassed by the gradually disappearing radiance that his people put a veil over him to hide his diminishing glow of glory, or *kabod*. Fearful that the glory of God had departed him, he began to doubt his abilities. Moses was concerned that he might become less impressive among the people he was trying to lead.

70

HOW IS YOUR *KABOD* THESE DAYS?

10 Min	Start Time:
	End Time:

Teaching Points:

- Retell Paul's use of the story of Moses to talk about the power of the Holy Spirit to reinstate a sense of fading or lost worth.

- Use a worn or damaged coin to demonstrate the point (an old nickel or Silver Dollar).

- Teach them that it is more than dings, and worn-down pressure points on the coin. If you put an old coin on a digital scale, you can measure the difference. The worn coin really weighs less than the new coin. If you're talking gold or silver, it really is worth less!

- We can feel like the worn coin, and others can believe we are like the worn coin. Satan finds ways to tell us that we are the worn coin.

- Feeling like we've become "worth-less" or others viewing us as a "light-weight" can have an extremely disheartening effect. Our serving potential will be minimized to the degree that we leave those dings and worn areas of our lives unaddressed by the Lord. He can revitalize those areas!

Facilitator Notes:

Coins represent the principle of *"kabod" (weighty and worth-less)*

Until the mid-20th century, coins were often made of silver or gold, which were quite soft and prone to wear. This meant coins naturally got lighter (and thus less valuable) as they aged. Vendors didn't care what the mint markings were, or whose image was imprinted on the face. They just cared that a $5 gold coin had $5 worth of gold in it. They would weigh the coins to make sure they weren't getting "shortchanged!"

Over the years and the wear and tear of life, we can find ourselves being worn down or nicked-up. We can see ourselves, or create a perception with others, to be damaged goods. Like a worn nickel, as 3rd Stagers we can feel like we've become a lightweight—perhaps even worth *less* than in our younger days.

This creates a huge issue that MUST be addressed. If we feel worth *less*, then what is our remedy? Isaiah is a perfect example of a person who was awed by God, but felt that his surroundings in life, the events he had experienced, and the personal choices he had already made had *ruined* him.

Isaiah 6:1-8
In the year that King Uzziah died, I saw the Lord seated on a throne, high and exalted, and the train of His robe filled the temple. ²Above Him were seraphs, each with six wings: With two wings they covered their faces, with two they covered their feet, and with two they were flying. ³And they were calling to one another: "Holy, holy, holy is the Lord Almighty; the whole earth is full of His glory." ⁴At the sound of their voices the doorposts and thresholds shook and the temple was filled with smoke. ⁵"Woe to me!" I cried. "I am ruined! For I am a man of unclean lips, and I live among a people of unclean lips, and my eyes have seen the King, the Lord Almighty." ⁶Then one of the seraphs flew to me with a live coal in his hand, which he had taken with tongs from the altar. ⁷With it he touched my mouth and said, "See, this has touched your lips; your guilt is taken away and your sin atoned for." ⁸Then I heard the voice of the Lord saying, "Whom shall I send? And who will go for us?" And I said, "Here am I. Send me!"

Isaiah was awed by the overwhelming beauty and majesty of God—the Creator and King of Creation. But as he considered the worthiness of God while the angels worshiped, he became acutely aware of his own failures. He was overwhelmed with a sense of shame—his own personal worth-*less*-ness. What happened to Isaiah in this moment gives hope to those of us who have felt like we have lost our *kabod*!

God wants to address our sense of personal defacing/worth-*less*-ness. When we feel worn out, defaced, or lightweight, God desires to restore us to our full ***worth-i-ness***. So often, that happens in personal worship and confession. There is never a better environment than in worship to expect God to point out Earth's need, share His desire to rescue, and respond to your willingness to understand your call. Our goal is to get

71

ISAIAH 6:1-8

⏳ 5 Min	Start Time:
	End Time:

Teaching Points:

- Read the passage and trace the emotions of Isaiah throughout the story.

- Particularly mark the swing from awe to awful and the impact of his sense of sin.

- Take the time to stop and pray for anyone feeling dinged, damaged, or de-valued.

ACT3 Participant Guide

to the point that we realize our *kabod* has been restored, and that, like Isaiah, we excitedly and passionately wave our hand in the air, shouting, "Send Me! Send Me!"

TABLE TALK

Becoming a 3rd stager can bring with it a feeling that you're losing *kabod*! Spend some time and share about the circles of life where you feel worth a little less than you once did.

AN OLD STORY, A NEW PERSPECTIVE

There was once a velveteen rabbit, and in the beginning, he was really splendid. He was fat and bunchy, as a rabbit should be; his coat was spotted brown and white, he had real thread whiskers, and his ears were lined with pink sateen.

For a long time he lived in the toy cupboard or on the nursery floor, and no one thought very much about him. He was naturally shy, and being only made of velveteen, some of the more expensive toys quite snubbed him.

Between them all, the poor little Rabbit was made to feel himself very insignificant and commonplace, and the only person who was kind to him at all was the Skin Horse.

The Skin Horse had lived longer in the nursery than any of the others. He was so old that his brown coat was bald in patches and showed the seams underneath, and most of the hairs in his tail had been pulled out to string bead necklaces. He was wise, for he had seen a long succession of mechanical toys arrive to boast and swagger, and by-and-by break their mainsprings and pass away, and he knew that they were only toys, and would never turn into anything else. For nursery magic is very strange and wonderful, and only those playthings that are old and wise and experienced like the Skin Horse understand all about it.

"What is REAL?" asked the Rabbit one day, when they were lying side by side near the nursery.

"Real isn't how you are made," said the Skin Horse. "It's a thing that happens to you. When a child loves you for a long, long time, not just to play with, but REALLY loves you, then you become Real."

"Does it hurt?" asked the Rabbit.

"Sometimes," said the Skin Horse, for he was always truthful. "When you are Real, you don't mind being hurt."

72

TABLE TALK

| ⧗ 10 Min | Start Time: |
| | End Time: |

AN OLD STORY, A NEW PERSPECTIVE

| ⧗ 7 Min | Start Time: |
| | End Time: |

Teaching Tips:

- Be prepared to read *The Velveteen Rabbit* smoothly and emotionally.

- Ask the participants to close their books and listen as you read.

- Read straight through and let the story speak for itself.

- Using the Velveteen Rabbit story is best used as a Going Deeper element if time is of any concern as you near the closing of the session.

"Does it happen all at once," he asked, "or bit by bit?"

"It doesn't happen all at once," said the Skin Horse. "You become. It takes a long time. That's why it doesn't happen often to people who break easily, or have sharp edges, or who have to be carefully kept. Generally, by the time you are Real, most of your hair has been loved off, and your eyes drop out and you get loose in the joints and very shabby. But these things don't matter at all, because once you are Real you can't be ugly, except to people who don't understand."

"I suppose *you* are real?" said the Rabbit. And then he wished he had not said it, for he thought the Skin Horse might be sensitive. But the Skin Horse only smiled.

"The Boy's Uncle made me Real," he said. "That was a great many years ago; but once you are Real you can't become unreal again. It lasts for always."

The Rabbit sighed. He longed to become Real, to know what it felt like; and yet the idea of growing shabby and losing his eyes and whiskers was rather sad. He wished that he could become it without these uncomfortable things happening to him.

One evening, when the Boy was going to bed, and his Nana was in a hurry, she said, "Here, take your old Bunny!" He'll do to sleep with you!" And she dragged the Rabbit out by one ear, and put him in the Boy's arms.

That night, and for many nights after, the Velveteen Rabbit slept in the Boy's bed. At first he found it rather uncomfortable, for the Boy hugged him very tight, and sometimes he rolled over on him, and sometimes he pushed him so far under the pillow that the Rabbit could scarcely breathe. But very soon he grew to like it, for the Boy used to talk to him, and made nice tunnels for him under the bedclothes that he said were like the burrows the real rabbits lived in. When the Boy dropped off to sleep, the Rabbit would snuggle down close under his little warm chin and dream, with the Boy's hands clasped close around him all night long.

And so time went on, and the little Rabbit was very happy—so happy that he never noticed how his beautiful velveteen fur was getting shabbier and shabbier, and his tail becoming unsewn, and all the pink rubbed off his nose where the Boy had kissed him.

And once, when the Boy was called away suddenly to go out to tea, the Rabbit was left out on the lawn until long after dusk, and Nana had to come and look for him with the candle because the Boy couldn't go to sleep unless he was there. He was wet through the dew. Nana grumbled as she rubbed him off with a corner of her apron.

"You must have your old Bunny!" she said. "Fancy all that fuss for a toy!"

The Boy sat up in bed and stretched out his hands.

"Give me my Bunny!" he said. "You mustn't say that. He isn't a toy. He's REAL!"

When the little Rabbit heard that, he was happy, for he knew that what the Skin Horse had said was true at last. The nursery magic had happened to him, and was a toy no

73

ACT3 Participant Guide

longer. He was REAL. The Boy himself had said it.

That night he was almost too happy to sleep, and so much love stirred in his little sawdust heart that it almost burst. And into his boot-button eyes, that had long ago lost their polish, there came a look of wisdom and beauty, so that even Nana noticed it next morning when she picked him up, and said, "I declare if that old Bunny hasn't got quite a knowing expression!"

The Skin Horse was right. Sometimes living and loving can be painful, but it is the only way to become real. The rabbit knew that now he must teach the other toys how to be real and to love their patches, sewn up places, and achy joints. Finally, the Velveteen Rabbit understood that being real is forever, and he still had a lot of work and living to do.

 HOMEWORK

- Have you had conversations that you intuitively sensed God was using to speak to you through a person? Recall the takeaways of those conversations and write them down. If appropriate, include them in the map of your **Journey** (p. 25).

- Spend some time prayerfully reflecting on the results of your **Spiritual Gifts Assessment** (p. 49). Record your top three **Spiritual Gifts** in your *Calling Star* (p. xiii).

- Complete the **People Worksheet** (p. 76).

- Spend some time prayerfully reflecting on your **People Worksheet** (p. 76) and the map of your **Journey** (p. 25). Ask the Holy Spirit to identify those who are speaking into your life now who may help you know the hope of your calling. Use the insights provided by Him to complete the **People** point of your *Calling Star* (p. xiii).

- Complete the **Passions Worksheet** (p. 92) and be ready to share during next week's group.

CLOSING PRAYER

HOMEWORK

5 Min	Start Time: End Time:

- Quickly cover the Homework assignments and emphasize the importance of keeping their *Calling Star* current.

ADDITIONAL NOTES: SPIRITUAL GIFTS

Additional Notes:

75

People Worksheet

Reflect on the following questions and write down your responses. Next week we will spend some time sharing one-on-one, as well as sharing around your table, some of your responses to these challenging yet critical questions.

- Who are the **People** that have played a role in your life that are comparable to those that Paul identifies in Timothy's life? Who has God used in the past to speak into your life?

- What was the impact of these **People** on your life?

- Have you ever sensed that God used someone to speak very specifically to you? What was the summary of the message(s)?

76

- Who is speaking into your life now that God can use to guide and encourage you as you discover your calling and obey Him by serving?

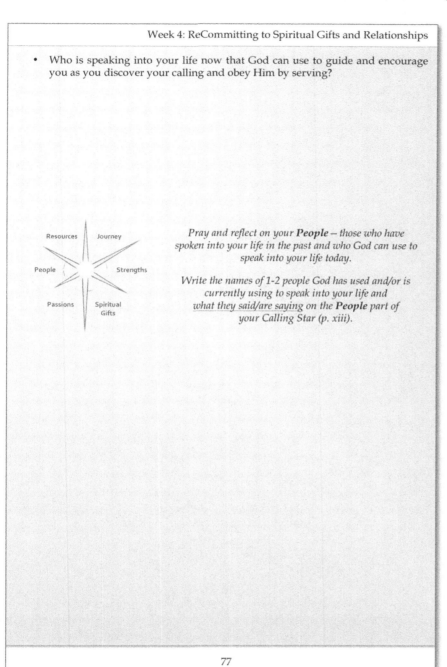

*Pray and reflect on your **People** — those who have spoken into your life in the past and who God can use to speak into your life today.*

*Write the names of 1-2 people God has used and/or is currently using to speak into your life and what they said/are saying on the **People** part of your Calling Star (p. xiii).*

77

ACT3 Participant Guide

78

ACT3 Participant Guide

78

Week 5 at a Glance
ReCalculating Your Passions and Resources

OUTCOMES

- Develop an understanding of personal passions in the search for the sweet spots of serving.
- Solidify the value of the participants' Spiritual Gifts through peer sharing.
- Establish the value of relationships in the Master's work.
- Reinstate a sense of personal worth for those suffering experiences that have dinged and scarred them.
- Continue to raise the value of finished homework and a completed *Calling Star*.

AGENDA

WELCOME AND OPENING PRAYER		
Group Discussion	• Share insights from People Worksheet	**Time:** Up to 6:15
The Master's Stroke that Creates a Fire of Passions in our Soul	• John 2:13-17 • A fire in the belly that's explainable	**Time:** 10 minutes
Table Talk	• Share learnings for Passion Worksheet	**Time:** 15 minutes
Your Real and Final Finish Line	• 2 Timothy 4:6-8 • Paul's Tour de Middle East and Europe	**Time:** 10 minutes
Personal Sharing	• What are the main tasks you've finished? • What God-projects are still unfinished?	**Time:** 10 minutes
BREAK		**Time: 15 minutes**
Resource of Time	• Psalms 90:10-12 • The challenges the psalmist addresses	**Time:** 10 minutes
Where does our Time Go?	• An anonymous example • Time categories and definitions	**Time:** 15 minutes
Group Discussion	• What are the observations of the example? • How has the use of your time evolved? • Do you anticipate balance in your study?	**Time:** 10 minutes
Resource of Skills	• Exodus 31:1-6 • The distinction of **Skills** and their potential	**Time:** 10 minutes
Personal Accountability	• 2 Corinthians 5:10 • The Bema Seat and a high-five moment	**Time:** 10 minutes

Homework	• Complete **Passions** point of the *Calling Star* • Complete Time and Skills Worksheet. Add results to **Resources** point of the *Calling Star* • Complete Serving Exploration Worksheet	**Time:** 5 minutes

Week 5: ReCalculating Your Passions and Resources

OPENING PRAYER

 GROUP DISCUSSION
*'Aha' from homework: the **People** point of your Calling Star*

We've come to depend on the technology of GPS to get us from where we are to where we want to be, particularly when we're traveling in new land, or the route is complicated. Not only can it set our course to the desired destination, it can *recalculate* our course after we've made a wrong turn, or missed a right one. Sometimes we drift. Sometimes we encounter a detour. And sometimes we get careless or distracted. No matter the journey, course corrections are a part of travel and we must always find a way to get back on track. Whether it's the voice of the GPS or another person telling you to recalculate, there is something reassuring when you know there is course correction in process.

There are two points to the *Calling Star* that we will consider in this session. The first is **Passions**, and the second is **Resources**. Both points can experience drift, distraction, and even detours. Both shed light on the pathway that leads to finding opportunities to serve

> *"If you can't figure out your purpose, figure out your passion. For your passion will lead you right into your purpose."*
>
> T.D. Jakes

in alignment with your calling. Recalculating your **Passions** and **Resources** can add powerful lumens to your *Calling Star*.

79

Reminders:

- Start discussion as close to the designated starting time as possible.

- As you welcome, remind the group of our purpose: *To connect 3rd Stagers to people and opportunities to serve in alignment with their calling.*

GROUP DISCUSSION

- Use up to 7-8 minutes for group discussion of personal "aha insights" from their People worksheet and the People point of their *Calling Star.*

ACT3 Participant Guide

PASSIONS

The good things that make your heart sing and the bad things that break your heart

John 2:13-17

When it was almost time for the Jewish Passover, Jesus went up to Jerusalem. 14In the temple courts he found men selling cattle, sheep and doves, and others sitting at tables exchanging money. 15So he made a whip out of cords, and drove all from the temple area, both sheep and cattle; he scattered the coins of the money changers and overturned their tables. 16To those who sold doves he said, "Get these out of here! How dare you turn my Father's house into a market!" 17His disciples remembered that it is written: "Zeal for your house will consume me."

In this context, the word *zeal* means to be hot, fervent; it is the capacity or state of passionate commitment. We describe a passionate person as someone who is *on fire*.

Let's hit pause and do a quick remedial middle school science lesson. The Universe is made up of matter and energy. Matter is made up of atoms and molecules (groupings of atoms) and energy causes the atoms and molecules to always be in motion - either bumping into each other or vibrating back and forth. The motion of atoms and molecules creates a form of energy called heat. The more energy you introduce to the particles, the faster they move and the more frequently the bump into each other. The more frequently they bump into each other, the more heat they generate. WHEW!

Now lets apply this kid's science lesson to what happens when God builds a fire in our belly. He stokes those fires in three basic steps:

- First, God gives us a new heart with the core values consistent with the Kingdom of God.

- Next, He infuses us with His supernatural power by giving us His Holy Spirit. When Jesus promised us that the Holy Spirit would come, He said that the Spirit would give us power. The Greek word we translate with the English *power* is *dunamis. Dunamis* is the word from which we derive our word *dynamite.* So, we're talking an infusion of supernatural energy into our souls.

- Lastly, He opens our eyes to the realities of the injustices and brokenness of our world.

The presence of Holy Spirit power energizes our core values and they begin to smack into the heart-moving brokenness of the world around us. The bumping of our core

80

PASSIONS

⧗	**10 Min**	Start Time: End Time:

BIG IDEA

The Biblical word is translated from a concept of "fire in the belly." Jesus in the Temple is the example. He didn't simply get mad; He was angry that the money exchangers were impeding the purpose of the Temple as a house of prayer *and He took bold action.* **Passions** may well serve as one of the brightest points of your *Calling Star.*

DESIRED OUTCOME

- To charge people to consider if the fire in their belly burns for their own purposes, or if It burns for the benefit of others.

- To encourage people to look for those serving opportunities that seem to light a fire in their soul, while teaching that God, as the Master Creator, uniquely energizes us for the works He has prepared for us to do.

Teaching Points:

- There are two points to the *Calling Star* that we will consider in this session. The first is **Passions**, and the second is **Resources.**

- The Greek word translated as "zeal" paints the picture of a "fire in the belly."

- Not all passions are healthy ones! But those in which the Holy Spirit lights the fire are forces that change the world.

- Passions often serve to provide some of the brightest lumens in the search for opportunities to serve in alignment with a 3rd Stager's calling.

- Passion is a mature trait inasmuch as it generally results from natural talents, life experiences, and ways of thinking that smack into the problems and issues of a broken world. A fire in the belly can't be contained by sympathetic feelings. Something must be done!

- Many times, a fire in the belly provides the "steam power" that becomes an unstoppable force when confronted with the challenges of serving.

TABLE TALK

⧖	**15 Min**	Start Time:
		End Time:

Week 5: ReCalculating Your Passions and Resources

values into the brokenness of the world around us causes a metaphorical heat—or fire—in the belly. The Greeks referred to that *"fire in the belly"* as **Passion**.

The disciples recognized the presence and power of a personal passion in Jesus when He saw the abuses that were taking place in the Temple. They saw that it was *eating Him alive*. Jesus couldn't stand the thought that His Father's house was less than God intended; and He couldn't live with those abuses He witnessed which dishonored His Father and hurt people. You are created in God's image. You are no exception to having the God-designed capacity to burn with a passion.

> *"The place God calls you is the place where your deep gladness and the world's deep hunger meet."*
>
> Frederick Buechner, American writer and theologian

So, one of the ways God raises His voice to clarify His call in our lives is to build a fire in our belly, or give us **Passions**.

TABLE TALK

- Discuss the responses you completed in the **Passions Worksheet** (p. 92).

- What did you learn about your gladness and your **Passion** from your reflections on what makes your heart sing?

- What did you learn about what breaks your heart?

- What surprised you?

81

ACT3 Participant Guide

RETHINKING YOUR FINISH LINE

2 Timothy 4:6-8
For I am already being poured out like a drink offering, and the time has come for my departure. ⁷I have fought the good fight, I have finished the race, I have kept the faith. ⁸Now there is in store for me the crown of righteousness, which the Lord, the righteous Judge, will award to me on that day - and not only to me, but also to all who have longed for His appearing.

The **Tour de France** is an annual multi-stage bicycle race, primarily held in France. The race consists of 21 segments (stages) over a 23-day period, covering around 2,200 miles. While the route changes each year, the format stays the same: the aggressive racing and risk-taking, the time trials, the passage through the mountain chains of the Pyrenees and the Alps, and the finish in Paris.

Paul had been living his own "Tour de Middle East/Europe," completing many painstaking, miraculous segments in jaw-dropping fashion. He had traveled the known world. He carried the Gospel to Western civilization. He had completed multiple missionary journeys and established churches across two continents. He had written 12 books of the New Testament and was penning his last with the words we read. He had discipled a generation of people who had the reigns of spiritual leadership in their hands. His list of finished legs of his journey was long and impressive. Yet Paul's life-long journey had but one **finish line** in view.

PERSONAL SHARING

- What are the main tasks of your life that you would describe as basically finished?

- What are the markers you'll use to confirm that you are truly finished with your calling?

- What God-planned projects do you want to finish between here and there?

82

RETHINKING YOUR FINISH LINE

| ⏳ 10 Min | Start Time:
End Time: |

BIG IDEA

There is but one finish line. If we are not careful, we can get comfortable with the thought of being "finished," because we have finished a leg of the race — but not the race itself. Definitely enjoy the accomplishments and joys of each leg of your race, but don't go to sleep and miss the cumulative crescendo of the journey. You've got momentum. Don't lose it!

DESIRED OUTCOME

- To help people note and celebrate the legs of their journey that are finished, while urging them on to run the next legs of their race with the same determination and level of excellence.

- For those who wish they had run the earlier legs better, remind them that the 3rd Stage of life provides beautiful opportunities to gain ground in fulfilling and exciting ways. This season gives us all time and opportunity to finish well!

Teaching Points:

- Read 2 Timothy 4:6-8 and ask the group to circle the word "race" in the verse.

- Briefly note Paul's "Tour de Middle East/Europe" and his completed list:

  o Traveled the known world

  o 1st to carry the Gospel to the Western Civilization

  o Completed multiple missionary journeys, and established churches across two continents

  o Wrote 12 books of the NT and was penning his last with the words we read

  o Discipled a generation who would lead the church after he was gone

- All this was completed but he had not considered himself finished until his realization that he was close to the "bottom of the drink offering!"

Facilitator Notes:

- Personal story…

PERSONAL SHARING

| 10 Min | Start Time: |
| | End Time: |

BREAK

 RESOURCES
A source of supply that can be drawn upon in order to achieve a desired outcome

No discovery process can be complete when searching for God's calling for your life without due diligence to consideration of the personal resources of your **Time** and **Skills**. People stumble at the door of opportunity when they make uninformed decisions about their availability. Identifying your skills can be like putting on prescription glasses when looking at opportunities to serve.

TIME: *The 168 hours available to you each week and how you use them*

Every day is a gift from the Father of Life. How many days you have is on God. How those days are spent is on you. Time is a factor in your serving equation and must be put on the table when sincerely looking at where God is calling you to serve.

> *"The bad news is time flies. The good news is you're the pilot."*
>
> Michael Altshuler

God has blessed each one of us with a complex love/hate relationship with **Time**. Especially as a 3rd Stager, you are faced with a simple (but not easy) question, "Where are you devoting your time and energy?"

 Psalms 90:10-12
As for the days of our life, they contain seventy years, or if due to strength, eighty years, yet their pride is but labor and sorrow; For soon it is gone and we fly away. [11]Who understands the power of Your anger and Your fury, according to the fear that is due You? [12]So teach us to number our days, that we may present to You a heart of wisdom. (NASU)

These are the words of an exemplary 3rd Stager: Moses. He was fully engaged in what was an obvious 3rd season of his life, leading the Children of Israel and helping them get to their Promised Land.

His life was robust, both as a boy and young man in the Egyptian palaces, and as a 2nd Stager; making a life on his own, discovering all the facets of his character, and

BREAK

⧗ **15 Min**	Start Time: End Time:

RESOURCES

⧗ **10 Min**	Start Time: End Time:

BIG IDEA

One of the two primary elements of the 3rd Stage of life is discretionary time. At no stage of life does the length of the day change. There are 24 hours in every day of your life, regardless of how busy you are or how fast they fly by. Many 3rd Stagers report being "busier than they've ever been." And that is feasibly true. The issue is that now they have a choice as to how busy they are and how they choose to spend their *discretionary time*.

DESIRED OUTCOME

- To help participants get a clearer sense as to where their time is being spent.

- To encourage them to make adjustments that seem prudent.

- To help them ascertain how much discretionary time they might have to invest in serving opportunities.

Teaching Points:

- Remind them that there are 168 hours in every person's week.

- Moses: the exemplary 3rd Stager.

- Read Psalms 90:10-12.

- Ask the participants to circle the words "teach us to number our days."

  o Living like our days are numbered is not natural (teach us!)

  o Making the most of those days is not simple (so that we will yield hearts of wisdom)

  o We are accountable to God for how we live our days (gift to you)

  o Encourage them to close their eyes and invite the Holy Spirit to teach them to number their days

ACT3 Participant Guide

preparing for the God-designed calling on his life after he left Egypt to lead his family and friends to the Promised Land.

In these three short verses, Moses acknowledges that even his own high profile, experience-packed life will come to an end and that he will experience what we all face – THE EXIT. Not only does Moses address the seriousness of God's estimation of us and our response to Him, he then goes beyond asking God to help him be keenly aware that he only has so many days to live. Moses teaches us to live each day with wisdom, no matter the number of our days, seeing life from God's point of view.

Psalms 90:10-12 teaches us at least three valuable lessons:

- Living like our days are numbered is not _____. (Teach us!)

- Making the most of those days is not _____. (So that we will yield hearts of wisdom.)

- We are _____to God for how we live our days. (Gift to You.)

GETTING HONEST ABOUT YOUR TIME

Are you serious about discovering God's calling for your life as a 3rd Stager? If so, it must include taking an HONEST look in the mirror to see how you are REALLY spending your time. It takes asking the tough questions. It means examining your heart to make sure that your time is spent wisely doing what is important, meaningful, and purposeful to God's plan for you.

> "It's not enough to be busy, so are the ants. The question is, what are we busy about?"
>
> Henry David Thoreau

84

GETTING HONEST ABOUT YOUR TIME

15 Min	Start Time:
	End Time:

Teaching Points:

- Below is the example (table and chart) of the use of **Time** in a 168-hour week.

  o Go through example

  o Answer questions – this will be their homework

- Emphasize: The **Time** point of our *Calling Star* is continually changing and transitioning as we walk our own personal journey. Know that adjusting your time and schedule is a normal and needful part of our walk.

- Lots of people have opinions of how you spend your time, but you are finally accountable to only One!

Week 5: ReCalculating Your Passions and Resources

Here is an example of the use of **Time** in a 168-hour week:

	Mon	Tue	Wed	Thur	Fri	Sat	Sun	Weekly Total
Rest/Sleep	6	6	6	6	8	8	6	46
Work	0	4	4	4	0	0	0	12
Leisure	3	2	2	2	6	6	4	25
Family	2	2	2	2	3	4	3	18
Mealtime	2	2	2	2	2	2	2	14
Personal Care	1	1	1	1	1	1	1	7
Maintenance/Chores	1	1	1	1	1	1	4	10
Wellness	1	0	1	0	1	0	0	3
Social World	1	1	1	1	2	2	2	10
Devotional Life	2	0.5	0.5	0.5	0	0	2	5.5
Serving	1	0	0	0	0	0	0	1
Travel	0	1	1	1	0	0	0	3
Unaccounted	4	3.5	2.5	3.5	0	0	0	13.5
Daily Total	24	24	24	24	24	24	24	168

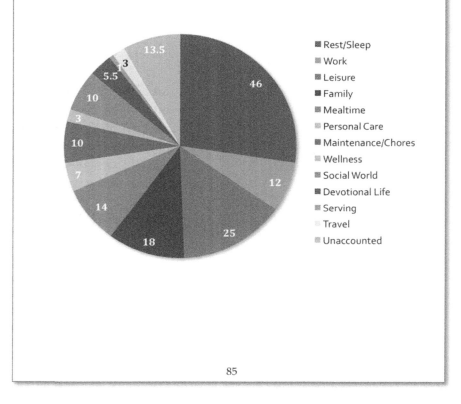

- Rest/Sleep
- Work
- Leisure
- Family
- Mealtime
- Personal Care
- Maintenance/Chores
- Wellness
- Social World
- Devotional Life
- Serving
- Travel
- Unaccounted

85

ACT3 Participant Guide

TIME CATEGORIES & DEFINITIONS

1. **Rest/Sleep:** Night time sleeping, naps, or general resting time that does NOT fit into other categories below

2. **Work:** Office hours, prep time (commute is under travel)

3. **Leisure:** Reading, hobbies, TV, or general 'alone' time recharging

4. **Family:** Nuclear family time, spouse time, dating time, support of child/grandchild, support, babysitting, aging parent care

5. **Mealtime:** Prep, eating, planning

6. **Personal Care:** Bathing, grooming, professional services

7. **Maintenance/Chores:** Household chores, shopping, property upkeep, personal finances

8. **Wellness:** Exercise, medical services

9. **Social World:** Friend time, social media

10. **Devotional Life:** Prayer, weekend worship, daily devotions, Bible studies

11. **Serving:** Church volunteerism, community volunteerism

12. **Travel/Commute:** Time spent traveling to/from places including work

13. **Unaccounted:** Remaining free time available

GROUP DISCUSSION

- What observations can you make from looking at this **Time** example?

- In general, how has your **Time** evolved as a 3rd Stager compared to other times in your life?

- Is there an area in your life that you anticipate is out of balance where you are spending either too much time or not enough?

86

GROUP DISCUSSION

10 Min	Start Time:	
	End Time:	

SKILLS: *The ability to do something well; expertise*

A cursory look at **Skills** may make them seem as something less than spiritual. Not true! The Bible is full of powerful examples of people with certain skills being used by God to win the day. David was both a musician and a warrior. A family in Israel carried the genetics, mixed with a tragic life experience, which equipped them to be the skilled songwriters and worship leaders of Israel. Arguably, the most powerful statement of the role of skills in God's plans is recorded in Exodus 31. Like us, God wanted to make the choice on who built His house.

Exodus 31:1-6
Then the Lord said to Moses, [2]"See, I have chosen Bezalel… and I have filled him with the Spirit of God, with wisdom, with understanding, with knowledge and with all kinds of skills – [4]to make artistic designs for work in gold, silver and bronze, [5]to cut and set stones, to work in wood, and to engage in all kinds of crafts. [6]Moreover, I have appointed Oholiab…to help him. Also I have given ability to all the skilled workers to make everything I have commanded you."

Skills are distinct from **Strengths** and **Spiritual Gifts**. Yet they are still beautiful expressions of God's handiwork in our lives that are inexorably linked with all our other attributes.

Kyle Parton, CEO of Epiphany Publishing says, "I see strengths and skills are different in that perhaps strengths are related to how I'm wired and who I am, where skills are related to what I do. They're different in that the former is internal and the latter is external.

Although they're different, I think they have more in common than they have in contrast. What they share is that they both need to somehow reference *action* to be meaningful at all. I cannot think of a personality or heart trait that is meaningful independent of action. 'Oh, her strength is that she's a caretaker.' That means she's skilled at assessing needs and finding ways to meet them. 'His strength is that he's a people person.' That means he's skilled at rapport building, networking, storytelling, etc. Both of those traits are made more real and concrete through action.

Think about the role of action in other common strengths. Even an abstract strength like creativity is only meaningful when describeing what creative people can *do*. That is, what skills they have. They are skilled at envisioning original ideas, playfully connecting seemingly unrelated concepts, breaking out of common mental routines and patterns,

> "It is possible to fly without motors, but not without knowledge and skill."
>
> Wilbur Wright

SKILLS

| 15 Min | Start Time: |
| | End Time: |

Teaching Points:

- Note the Biblical value of skills.

- Read Exodus 31:1-6.

- Skills are limitless in possibilities. For example, they can range from calligraphy to copyediting; from working with spreadsheets to IT; from being a mechanic to being a musician; and on and on.

- **Skills** may be the point of the *Calling Star* that most readily catches the attention of serving organizations.

- Skills can serve to lead you where you are called, or they could feel overused and leave the participant looking for something fresher.

brainstorming, etc. These descriptions are all built around *verbs*. Furthermore, if they don't have these skills, then I would argue that creativity isn't one of their strengths. So, my point is that **Strengths** and **Skills** are easily grouped by considering their dependent relationship to action. To depict it graphically…"

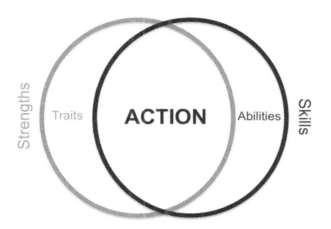

This entire Discovery experience is meant to lead to action in your next God-sized calling. Do you believe Paul was right? He said, *For we are God's masterpiece. He has created us anew in Christ Jesus, so we can do the good things He planned for us long ago.* The Master Painter has blended the beauties of our **Skills** into the complete picture of *who* He has made us to **be**. And *who* He has made us to **be** is a huge indicator of *what* He has called us to **do**.

It would be incongruous to believe that God positioned us in life to develop **Skills** that He had no plans to use. So take inventory of your **Skills**. Expect them to lead to action. And don't be surprised if the action nut doesn't fall far from the calling tree!

RETHINKING YOUR ULTIMATE ACCOUNTABILITY TO GOD

Analogous to our own judicial system with its many different courtrooms and their purposes, the Bible describes two distinctly different courtrooms in Heaven.

The first of the two courtrooms referenced in Heaven is noted by Paul in 2 Corinthians 5:10. It is called the Bema Seat and gives believers the opportunity to account for how they used the resources God entrusted to them. The second courtroom is referenced by John in Revelation 20:11. It is called the Great White Throne and

RETHINKING YOUR ULTIMATE ACCOUNTABILITY TO GOD

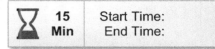

⧗	15 Min	Start Time: End Time:

Teaching Points:

- As with our court systems where each court serves a specific purpose in pursuing justice, there are two courtrooms in heaven; each has its purpose.

- Read 2 Corinthians 5:10.

- In contrast to the White Throne Judgment in Revelation 20:11 where the purpose is to call those who rejected Jesus into account for their sins, the Bema Seat of 1 Corinthians 5:10 has as its purpose the setting in which Jesus can celebrate what you accomplished with the life He redeemed and gave you. It is a high-five moment between believers and Jesus!

- Emphasize that the purpose of the Bema Seat is only for the rewarding of faithful believers.

- Encourage them to think about that beautiful moment when Jesus says, "Well done, good and faithful servant!" Challenge them to think about the kinds of things they want Jesus to applaud and what steps they might need to take to make it happen.

Week 5: ReCalculating Your Passions and Resources

calls unbelievers to account for their sin.

2 Corinthians 5:10
For we must all appear before the judgment seat of Christ, that each one may receive what is due him for the things done while in the body, whether good or bad.

Without the Light of Grace, reading this verse can send a shiver up the spine. How much more daunting does it get than the thought of standing before THE Judge and having some form of DVR revealing a play-by-play account of our life on the Big Screen.

The two verses cited in this segment make it difficult for even the most contentious to argue the clarity of the statements. Like all of Scripture, you have to decide if it's true. But it's hard to debate the word *all*. And the word is used in both passages. The operative question is *which* all do these passages address?

As already noted, The Great White Throne scene described in Revelation 20:11 is a setting that is judicial and punitive. The *all* are those who are identified in verse 5 as *the rest of the dead*. This *all* stands in contrast to those in verse 6, described as *blessed*, and having previously participated in the *first resurrection*. As believers, we are part of the verse 6 crowd, making us one of the *all* of 2 Corinthians 5:10.

The context of 2 Corinthians 5:10 involves Paul's stated personal goal in verse 9 *to please Him* (Jesus). The purpose of the Bema Seat of Christ is celebratory and rewarding. This is the happy *High-Five-from-Jesus* atmosphere when He tells you "Well done" loudly enough that the rest of us get to hear it! Paul told the Corinthian believers that the thought motivated him to serve Christ. Then he used the thought to motivate his friends to serve Christ as well.

You can feel like the little boy who couldn't wait to get home and show mommy his perfect score on his spelling test. ACT3 is designed to help you feel good about your spelling test and anticipate the moment you show Jesus!

REFLECTION:

How would that courtroom scene go for you if it were to happen tomorrow? How would you like for it to go? What steps might you take to alter the proceedings?

89

HOMEWORK

| | 5 Min | Start Time:
End Time: |

ACT3 Participant Guide

HOMEWORK

- Spend some time prayerfully reflecting on your **Passions Worksheet** (p. 92). Ask the Holy Spirit to show you which areas He is calling you to focus on in this next season of life. Use the insights provided by Him to complete the **Passions** point of your *Calling Star* (p. xiii).

- Complete the **Time Worksheet** (p. 94). Spend some time prayerfully reflecting on your **Time** distribution as it stands today. Ask the Holy Spirit to make clear to you how He wants you to redistribute your **Time** moving forward. Use the insights provided by Him to complete the **Time** contribution to the **Resources** point of your *Calling Star* (p. xiii).

- You will be emailed an Excel-based **Time Study Pie Chart**. Use either this electronic tool OR the paper **Time Worksheet Tool** provided (p. 94), which will help you gather the information manually.

- Complete the **Skills Worksheet** (p. 98). Spend some time prayerfully reflecting on the **Skills** you have developed through training and experience. Ask the Holy Spirit to make clear to you how He may want you to use your **Skills** moving forward. Use the insights provided by Him to complete the **Skills** contribution to the **Resources** point of your *Calling Star* (p. xiii).

- Complete the **Serving Exploration Worksheet** (p. 99).

NEXT WEEK IS OUR COACHING SESSION

We are excited to see what God has in store for this next chapter of your life because of your participation in this ACT3 Discovery Growth Group...

Please make sure you bring with you a completed copy of your Serving Exploration Worksheet and your completed *Calling Star*. These will be the two primary tools you'll reference during your coaching session.

CLOSING PRAYER

90

Week 5: ReCalculating Your Passions and Resources

ADDITIONAL NOTES:

91

Passions Worksheet

Reflect on the following questions and write down your responses. Next week we will spend some time sharing one-on-one and as a group some of our responses to these challenging yet critical questions.

WHAT MAKES YOUR HEART SING?

- What gives you "deep gladness?" It could be a task, area, or impact you have experienced.

- What is so meaningful to you that you would do it for free?

- If time and money were no object, what would you do for God?

- Name ONE task you would stay up all night to complete. It is those passions you find yourself saying, "I lose all track of time when I am engaged in…"

- What activities make you want to get out of bed in the morning?

- What is something you will talk about to anyone who will listen?

WHAT BREAKS YOUR HEART?

Circle the below issues that break your heart

3rd world countries	Elderly	Impoverished children	Poverty
Abuse	Financial instability	Isolation	Prison/reentry
Access to resources	Health crisis	Lack of clean water	Single parents
Addiction	Homelessness	Literacy	Veterans
Disabilities	Hunger	Loneliness	Widows/Widowers
Education	Illness	Mental illness	Other: _____

What else breaks your heart?

If there was one problem in the world that you could fix today, it would be:

Resources | Journey

People | Strengths

Passions | Spiritual Gifts

*Pray and reflect on your **Passions**, asking God to show you which areas He is calling you to focus on in this next season of life.*

*Write your top 1 or 2 **Passions** (with notes) on your Calling Star (p. xiii).*

93

Time Worksheet

Prayerfully reflect on the following questions and write down your responses. Next week we will open by sharing some of our responses and 'ahas' to these challenging yet critical questions.

- What are the top three categories of life that dominate your time, such as family, work, chores, and leisure?

- What is the one thing you would like to do, but seem to have the most challenge with fitting it in? Why?

- How much time is God leading you to commit to living out your calling by serving?

- What changes do you intentionally need to make to fulfill your calling?

TIME DISTRIBUTION

The following table and chart will be provided to you electronically in an Excel document entitled "TIME DISTRIBUTION." We recommend completing this exercise in the Excel document. Alternatively, you may manually complete the table below and use the pie chart to shade in your various distribution of time.

- Reflect on the following categories of time

- Fill in the estimated number of hours you typically spend each day in each category

TIME CATEGORIES & DEFINITIONS

1. **Rest/Sleep**: Night time sleeping, naps, or quiet times
2. **Work:** Office hours, prep time (commute is under travel)
3. **Leisure:** Reading, hobbies, TV, or general 'alone' time recharging
4. **Family:** Nuclear family time, spouse time, dating time, support of child/grandchild activities, babysitting, aging parent care
5. **Mealtime:** Prep, eating, planning
6. **Personal Care:** Bathing, grooming, professional services
7. **Maintenance/Chores:** Household chores, shopping, property upkeep, personal finances
8. **Wellness:** Exercise, medical services
9. **Social World:** Friend time, social media
10. **Devotional Life:** Prayer, weekend worship, daily devotions, Bible studies
11. **Serving:** Church volunteerism, community volunteerism
12. **Travel/Commute:** The time spent traveling to/from places including work
13. **Unaccounted:** Remaining free time available

	Mon	Tue	Wed	Thur	Fri	Sat	Sun
Rest/Sleep							
Work							
Leisure							
Family							
Mealtime							
Personal Care							
Maintenance/Chores							
Wellness							
Social World							
Devotional Life							
Serving							
Travel							
Unaccounted							
Daily Total							

Daily Total should = 24

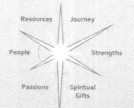

Pray and reflect on your **Time**, *asking God to show you how He is calling you to serve in this next season of life.*

Write your new serving commitment (in hours per week) on the **Resources** *part of your Calling Star (p. xiii). Be sure to leave room for* **Skills** *there as well.*

95

EACH SEGMENT IS 2 HOURS OF A 168-HOUR WEEK

1. Color a segment for each 2 hours spent per a category during the typical week. Use the number of segments necessary to reflect the total allocation of time used according to your Time Study.
2. Use a different shade or color for each of the 13 categories tracked in your Time Study.
3. Split any segment in half to account for the need to reflect 1-hour considerations. For an example: 11 hours for a particular category would require 5 of the 2 hour segments being colored, plus an additional ½ of a segment to accurately reflect your Time Study. The remaining ½ will be used by another 1-hour consideration that will result with another category.

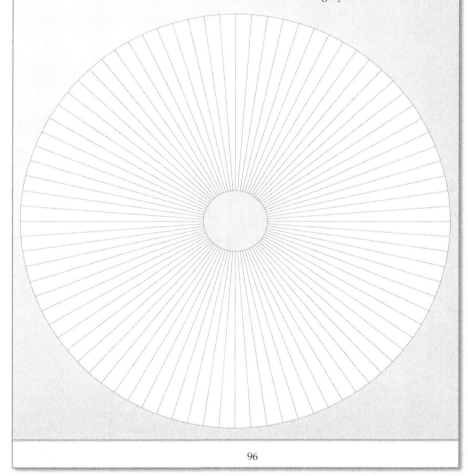

Week 5: ReCalculating Your Passions and Resources

ADDITIONAL NOTES:

Skills Worksheet

Reflect on the following questions and write down your responses. Next week we will spend some time sharing one-on-one, as well as sharing around your table, some of your responses to these challenging yet critical questions.

- What are some **Skills** you possess that have been instrumental in your **Journey** so far:

    o   Professionally?

    o   Personally?

    o   Recreationally?

- What **Skills** are you hoping to continue (or start) to use as you serve in this next season of life?

- What type of role (or action) might you serve in various ministries using your **Skills**?

Pray and reflect on your Skills. Ask God to show you how He has designed you to leverage these Skills to serve in His Kingdom.

Write your key 1-2 Skills or possible Roles you might fill on the Resources part of your Calling Star (p. xiii). Be sure to leave room for Time (your serving commitment) there as well.

Serving Exploration Worksheet

One of the most important components of ACT3 is the final connection between knowing the hope of your calling and serving His Kingdom accordingly. While you may not have all of the answers just yet, our hope is that you can now begin to think through the following questions prayerfully and with greater insight and knowledge of yourself, your strengths, gifts, and experiences that make you uniquely and wonderfully made.

> *"If God is your partner, make your plans BIG!"*
> D.L. Moody
>
> *"Sympathy is no substitute for action"*
> David Livingston

Prayerfully reflect on each point of your *Calling Star*

- Which point(s) are shining brightest as you think about serving in this season of life?

- Is there a point that is still unclear to you? If so go back to the worksheet for that point and identify the areas that are uncertain, unclear, or uncomfortable. Prayerfully reflect on the questions and your initial answers, asking God to show you what He wants you to know about this point of your *Calling Star* as it relates to your calling.

- Dare to dream. If time and money were no object, what would you do for God?

- How could you now combine your **Talents**, **Spiritual Gifts**, **Passions**, and **Resources** to fulfill your calling?

ACT3 Participant Guide

> *"This is our time on the history line of God. This is it. What will we do with the one deep exhale of God on this earth? For we are but a vapor and we have to make it count. We're on. Direct us, Lord, and get us on our feet."*
>
> Beth Moore

After you have reviewed your *Calling Star*, take some time to prayerfully complete the questions below. You will discuss your responses during your coaching session.

- The most impactful thing that I learned or discovered by being part of this ACT3 Discovery Growth Group is:

- The points of my *Calling Star* that are the strongest driver of my serving direction for this next season of life are:

- The specific serving commitment(s) that I will explore, begin, or continue are:

  o The action(s) that I will take to begin to follow-through on exploring these opportunities and commitments are:

  o What I still need to know/understand/decide to begin to pursue my calling is:

  o The resources/people who I will bring alongside to help me are:

Week 7: ReEngaging Your Calling

OPENING PRAYER

THE FINALE...AND THE BEGINNING

Welcome to your final week of the ACT3 Discovery Growth Group. You should now be better equipped to take your next steps in connecting with people and opportunities to serve in alignment with God's calling. Your decision will not be a shot in the dark, because you now have the light of your *Calling Star* to help guide you.

You are where our Wise Men were when they looked up and saw their own Star for the last leg of their journey. They were leaving Jerusalem. Jesus was a couple of miles away in Bethlehem. They had never been closer, and their Star had never been brighter. We know how their story ended! No Nativity Set is complete without our celebration of the success of the Wise Men's journey.

You are where those Wise Men were when they left Herod's palace for the true King's presence. You've never been closer, and your *Calling Star* has never been brighter. We are excited with you. We want to celebrate together the brightness of your *Calling Star* and anticipate the next leg of your journey as a servant of the King!

INDIVIDUAL SHARING OF SERVING COMMITMENTS

Please CHOOSE ONE of the questions in your **Serving Exploration Worksheet** (p. 99) that you would like to share with the group.

101

Reminders:

- Start discussion as close to the designated starting time as possible.

- As you welcome, remind the group of our purpose: *To connect 3rd Stagers to people and opportunities to serve in alignment with their calling.*

Teaching Tips:

- Make the welcome brief and the schedule of the evening clear. Take 5 minutes to prepare the participants for their personal sharing.

- Ask one of the most comfortable and clear-spoken participants to lead the time of sharing. They will set the tone for the rest of the evening.

Notes from Participant Sharing:

ACT3 Participant Guide

COMMUNION

1 Corinthians 11:23-26
For I received from the Lord what I also passed on to you: The Lord Jesus, on the night he was betrayed, took bread, ²⁴and when he had given thanks, he broke it and said, "This is my body, which is for you; do this in remembrance of me." ²⁵In the same way, after supper he took the cup, saying, "This cup is the new covenant in my blood; do this, whenever you drink it, in remembrance of me." ²⁶For whenever you eat this bread and drink this cup, you proclaim the Lord's death until he comes.

It has been our great joy to walk alongside you for the past six weeks as we have answered God's call for us to share the vision of **ACT3: *Connecting 3rd Stagers to people and opportunities to serve in alignment with their calling.***

It is our hope that ACT3 has enabled you to discover and implement your uniquely designed calling and purpose for your own life…. It is our even greater hope that, as you go forth, your excitement and commitment to live out your calling will be contagious to those around you. *Imagine what our families, our church, our friends, and the world could be if every 3rd Stager began to earnestly seek and discover their own purpose and calling.*

That is our BIG dream. We pray it has also become yours!

CLOSING PRAYER OR BLESSING PRAYER FOR PARTICIPANTS

We Want to Hear from You!

You will be receiving a Feedback Questionnaire via email within the next week. Please complete it to help evaluate your ACT3 Discovery Growth Group experience. Thank YOU!

The ACT3 Core Team

102

OPTIONAL METHODS TO CELEBRATE TOGETHER

- Celebrating Communion together.

- The giving of a symbolic towel of serving. The towel could be embroidered with the ACT3 ministry name, the date of this celebration week of the Discovery Group, or potentially their personal name.

Teaching Tips:

- Remind your group the beauty of this celebration as we remember the Master Servant and commit our future to His service.

- Distribute the elements.

- Read the passage and then make any personal comments you think appropriate.

- Pray over the Bread and lead the group in taking it, reminding them that it represents the Body of Christ, and to take it in remembrance of Him.

- Pray over the Cup and lead them in taking it, reminding them that it represents the Blood of Jesus and our full atonement, and to take it in remembrance of Him.

THE SERVING TOWEL
(Not in the Participant Guide)

John 13:2-5 (NIV): "The evening meal was in progress, and the devil had already prompted Judas, the son of Simon Iscariot, to betray Jesus. Jesus knew that the Father had put all things under his power, and that he had come from God and was returning to God; so he got up from the meal, took off his outer clothing, and wrapped a towel around his waist. After that, he poured water into a basin and began to wash his disciples' feet, drying them with the towel that was wrapped around him."

Teaching Tips:

- Just before Jesus laid the foundation for the beautiful and powerful elements of the Communion service, He demonstrated His love for his disciples in a practical way.

- Washing feet was not a new practice for the disciples. The realities of sandals and walking on filthy roads required more than a welcome mat to wipe your shoes. Homeowners provided a way to wash feet for guests as more than a common courtesy or relaxing massage. Housewives were likely as conscious of their floors as we are of ours!

- The courtesy was to provide more than the basin of water and wash clothes. They also commonly provided a person to wash their feet for them.

- As can be easily imagined, that was not a volunteer position in that culture. The task was assigned to the lowest slave in the household staff. It would not have been fun or desirable.

- Because they were in a room provided by an owner that was not in attendance, the group was left with no "servant" they could assign.

- All of the disciples knew of the custom. Most of the disciples likely realized that they had dirty feet. None of the disciples gave a thought to providing for the service themselves. Rather, they were bickering over who was the big shot among them.

- In the environment, Jesus quietly got up, prepared a basin of water, wrapped Himself with a towel and began to wash each of the disciple's feet. It was shocking demonstration of servanthood.

- It was an even greater demonstration of love.

- The Servant's Towel is a beautiful reminder that we are most like Jesus when we wear the towel and serve the needs of others.

About the Authors

COURTNEY SALATI

Courtney Salati spent 15 years in Corporate America as a Human Resource and Talent Management Leader before venturing out as an independent Organizational & Leadership Development Consultant in 2016. Around the time of this transition, in a true "God string of events" Courtney was led to ACT3, a ministry that was still just a concept, and her calling to serve was clear. Ever since, Courtney—a "2nd Stager with markings of a 3rd Stager"—has been using her gifts and talents to help strategically and operationally launch ACT3. Her prayer is that ACT3 will someday help guide countless 3rd Stagers to people and opportunities to serve in alignment with their calling.

Courtney is married to Nathan and is step-mom to Parker (7), Raya (5) and Hadleigh (3). The Salati family resides in Westfield, Indiana and attends Northview Church.

JEFF & BECKY HARLOW

Jeff Harlow, with the unfailing support of his wife, Becky, pastored Crossroads Community Church in Kokomo, Indiana for 38 years. Their roles at Crossroads expanded from pastoring a handful of families to growing the church to over 3000 and reaching thousands across north central Indiana. As God prompted, Jeff led Crossroads through a successful succession plan, culminating with publishing his first book, *Dancing With Cinderella: Leading a Healthy Church Transition.*

Jeff is a visionary, strategic leader, driven to see things happen. Developing the con-

103

cepts and tools of ACT3 was the perfect opportunity for him to use those strengths and leverage his experience as a 3rd Stager. Becky has been indespensable throughout the process, as her strengths of hospitality and flexibility have always been the oil for the multitasking team.

When Jeff and Becky transitioned from Crossroads, they reached a mutual agreement that whatever God had next, it must be done together—and God let them keep their word. This new season of life with ACT3 has yielded the sweetest experiences of all their time serving together.

Jeff and Becky still reside where they have lived for all of their 44 years of marriage. Their multigenerational family farm in Tipton County was the perfect place to raise their 5 kids and to stretch the limits of fun with their 13 grandkids. It's there that they live out the precepts of ACT3 and lead their peers in rediscovering their calling in this this dynamic ministry.

About the Publisher

Epiphany Publishing, LLC is a private publishing company based in Indianapolis, IN. We are devoted to exploring catalysts for growth in the fields of religion, psychology, business, and human development.

Each year, Epiphany Publishing donates at least 25% of all its profits to nonprofit organizations that fight profound injustice—especially those atrocities that rob the innocent of their future. This includes the global sex trade, child soldiers forced to fight in war, and other forms of unthinkable oppression. We invite you to join us in partnering with luminous, restorative organizations like saribari.com, warchild.org, worldvision.org, and antislavery.org.

We are always interested in meeting new authors and reviewing promising manuscripts. If you've got a transformational message that you believe would be a good fit to publish with us, please introduce yourself at www.epiphanypublishing.us.

105

Made in the USA
Middletown, DE
10 January 2022